A Gift For:

_____

From:

_____

Married for Life

INSPIRATIONS FROM THOSE MARRIED 50 YEARS OR MORE

By
Russ L. Potter, II
Bill Morelan

Married for Life

Copyright © 2004 by The Concerned Group, Inc.

Published by Hallmark Gift Books, a division of Hallmark Cards, Inc., Kansas City, MO 64141
Visit us on the Web at Hallmark.com.

Reflections written by Robin Schmitt
Product developed by Bordon Books

ISBN 978-1-59530-329-5
BOK4385

Printed and bound in China

Dedication

Lovingly dedicated to Russell Potter, Sr.
and his wife, Virginia – married seventy-eight years!

You only get out of a marriage what you put into it.

Eldon & Ginny Phillips

Married: October 30, 1946
Belle Center, Ohio

Eldon and Ginny went to high school together. His first move:
he stole her shoes during a play rehearsal! "It took him eight years
to convince me to marry him," laughs Ginny.

※

A young entrepreneur starts with an idea for a unique, new product. He carefully lays plans for a start-up business, calculating revenues and expenses. He meets with consultants, accountants, and attorneys. He works hard to sell the concept to banks and investors to raise capital. In time he leases space, purchases equipment, and hires employees. Finally he is ready to begin. He works hard, pouring himself into the business, determined to make it succeed. And it thrives.

But does he now merely sit back, relax, and enjoy the fruit of his labor? No! He works harder than ever, while conjuring up ideas for improving efficiency, bettering customer relations, bolstering profits.

If a marriage is to last a lifetime, it requires the same level of devotion and energy. Both partners must give 100 percent. Each must be available to the other when needed, fully present, ready to listen, to talk, to act. Both spouses must pour their heart and soul into this enterprise, making whatever sacrifice necessary to ensure success.

Yet what an investment! The payoff is a rich, healthy, loving relationship that lasts. And everyone involved reaps countless rewards.

Sound good? Devote time and energy to your marriage.

Whoever sows generously will also reap generously.

2 Corinthians 9:6

Have fun just being together.

Arthur & Mabel Johnson

Married: October 22, 1920
Oklahoma City, Oklahoma

Arthur and Mabel met when he came to pick up his brother's engagement ring, which she was returning! "Six months later we were married," Mabel says, laughing. During their seventy-three years of marriage, they took lots of little day trips and numerous vacations.

※

A good, lasting marriage requires effort – but it takes fun too! King Solomon said, "I commend the enjoyment of life" (Ecclesiastes 8:15). Have a good time with your spouse. Enjoy each other's company. It doesn't take a lot of money to have fun if you think of creative ways to be lighthearted and playful together.

When was the last time you flew a kite? Grab a couple of inexpensive ones and head for the beach, where there always seems to be a steady breeze. Kick off your shoes and walk together along the shoreline until you find a good spot, then let the wind take your kites as high as they can go, while you and your spouse sit on the sand, relax, and watch them soar. Before you know it, the sun will be setting over the water, putting on a free light show to add to the fun.

As you reel in your kites, admiring the colors on the horizon, take a moment to reflect on the One who provides you with so many blessings. After all, who made the sand on the beach? Who created the air and the wind? Who made the water, the sky, the glorious sunset? Most of all, who fashioned and breathed to life the wonderful person with whom you delight to share it all?

Go ahead – have some fun!

God . . . gives us richly all things to enjoy.
1 Timothy 6:17 nkjv

Never get too old to hold hands.

Arnold & Hazel Morelan

Married: February 17, 1920

Iola, Kansas

Arnold and Hazel were high school sweethearts.
Known for their busy, loving hands, they "retired"
by opening up a gift shop where Arnold cast concrete yard
ornaments and Hazel stitched handmade quilts and dolls.

It starts with a tiny fist wrapped around a mother's finger. It continues with a young hand held gently in one much larger. It endures through puppy love, adolescent relationships, and courtship. And if we are wise, it extends into marriage, through middle age, beyond the golden years, to the very end of life.

Holding hands is one of the most intimate expressions of love between two human beings.

Don't ever let this beautiful act slip away from you. It's so much more than a gesture of affection, so much greater than a mere symbol of connection. It's an incredibly meaningful communication, a deep connection in and of itself. It requires no words; in fact, no words can convey such a profound message.

Why would two people ever stop holding hands? Perhaps it seems silly, somehow undignified, when we're older and have been married a long time. We may begin to think such things were meant only for young lovers and newlyweds. That's far from true! Besides its many other purposes, holding hands helps satisfy the basic human need for physical touch, a need we never outgrow.

Hold your spouse's hand throughout your life together; don't ever let it go until the day when you've fulfilled every marriage vow and finally release it from your grasp, placing it lovingly, trustingly into the hand of God.

I am always with you; you hold me by my right hand.
You guide me with your counsel,
and afterward you will take me into glory.

Psalm 73:23-24

11

Do everything you can to express your love.

Lennie & Victoria Shane

Married: January 29, 1938

Tujunga, California

A man of few words, Lennie's silence is beautifully balanced by his wife Victoria's shining sense of humor.

࿇

True love – everyone's searching for it. Singers sing about it. Poets write about it. Novelists weave stories about it. Artists immortalize it in a drawing, a painting, a sculpture. Filmmakers portray it in images larger than life.

But how do you know if you have it?

There are many ways for you and your spouse to express your love, many ways to show each other how deeply you care. You can say it with words, with candy and flowers, with diamonds and gold. All these ways are wonderful, all should be used, but none proves your hearts to be true. Not one guarantees the veracity of your love.

The only way to know if you have true love is to see whether it stands the test of time. Has it endured hardship, boredom, and pain? Has it weathered life's busyness? Has it withstood the pressures of job, family, and home, the stresses of midlife and old age? Time alone will tell.

If you're just embarking on the marriage path, you'll know the level of your commitment to each other by the way you live out your lives together day by day, expressing your love in every possible way through respecting each other, encouraging each other, and serving each other minute by minute, hour by hour.

You determine whether the love you have is true over time. But you begin now.

Let's not just talk about love; let's practice real love.
This is the only way we'll know we're
living truly, living in God's reality.

1 John 3:18-19 msg

Let life's experiences draw you closer together.

Herman & Mary Sue Davis

Married: October 5, 1943

Greenville, South Carolina

Herman and Mary Sue sat next to each other in high school band. "I played sax, she played flute – and we shared a music stand!" says Herman. Today they share many things, such as working together to compile the family genealogy.

※

When shaping a vessel, potters exert equal pressure with their hands on both the outside and the inside of the clay to prevent it from collapsing. After the clay dries, it is glazed and then placed in a fiery kiln. The intense heat perfects the clay by removing blemishes, strengthening it, and enhancing the paint colors. The once wet piece of clay is finally transformed into a beautiful and useful piece of pottery.

Marriage can be viewed as a similar work in progress. Like the clay, you and your spouse will constantly face various pressures from life – job changes, financial stress, parenting responsibilities, and the list goes on. To prevent your marriage from collapsing, you must respond to any external pressure with the internal pressure of a powerful relationship with the living God.

Just as clay is fired in a kiln, so will your marriage go through periods of intense heat. But remember that your heavenly Father is using these times to remove imperfections in your relationship and make it stronger and more beautiful. Face the difficult times together, and let the Lord mold and perfect your marriage, lifting you to higher levels of intimacy with each other and with Him.

O Lord, you are our Father. We are the clay,
you are the potter; we are all the work of your hand.

Isaiah 64:8

Never let a day go by without telling each other, "I love you."

Jack & Bernice Wein

Married: February 23, 1946

Trenton, Michigan

Jack and Bernice's sense of humor is legendary. "Bernice said if I bought one more car, I'd have to sleep in it," Jack says, grinning. "I told her a man should have more than one bedroom!" "Instead of arguing, let the man think he's the boss," Bernice says with a wink. "Eventually he'll come around to your way of thinking."

Every spouse has a deep need to feel cherished, valued, treasured. Daily reminders of love and affection will fill your hearts and lift your spirits, nurturing your relationship and causing it to thrive like a lush, well-tended, sunlit garden. And just as a beautiful flower garden harbors many colorful varieties of annuals and perennials, there are countless ways to express love.

A special favor, a helping hand with the chores. A card, a bouquet, a tasty treat. A touch, a hug, an impromptu slow dance. A listening ear, a real conversation. A shared memory, hearty laughter, a walk in the moonlight. A wink, a smile, a compliment. And don't forget to speak those three little words, "I love you!"

Words are powerful. They can build you up individually and strengthen you as a couple. They can encourage you and remind you of your lifelong commitment to each other, of the reasons why you chose to journey through this life together.

"I love you." Poets and songwriters of every age have searched for compelling words to communicate the depth of such emotion, but none has found a better way than this simple, heartfelt phrase. It never wears out and it never goes out of style. Take a moment to hold hands, gaze into each other's eyes, and whisper it today.

A word fitly spoken is like apples of gold
in pictures of silver.
Proverbs 25:11 kjv

17

Take the days one at a time. Soon fifty years will pass – but it won't seem like it.

Al & Evylyn Little

Married: March 3, 1946

Bellflower, Missouri

Al and Evylyn Little are committed Christians.
Al works as a chaplain for the Los Angeles County jails.
Evylyn loves spending time with little children.

※

A lifelong marriage is built day by day. It is made of days that seem momentous and days that seem mundane. Yet every one is important, every one indispensable. As you and your spouse live out each day to its fullest potential, sharing its joys and challenges, your days steadily join together like the masonry in a sturdy brick home, forming a relationship that is solid and secure. Such a relationship, built on the sure foundation of faith in God and commitment to each other no matter what the days may bring, will stand forever.

Take the days one at a time, but don't take them – or each other – for granted. Make the most of each twenty-four hours. Don't allow the past to become an anchor; rather, forgive each other for yesterday's offenses. And don't let worry about the future rob even one day of its joy; instead, put tomorrow in God's hands. When times get tough, continue to love, support, and encourage one another day by day, hour by hour, minute by minute, and trust the Lord to see you through. Before you know it, you and your beloved will be celebrating your golden anniversary – and wondering where the time went!

Oh, satisfy us early with Your mercy,
That we may rejoice and be glad all our days!
Psalm 90:14 nkjv

19

Love each other and share common goals.

Ray & Florence Borquez

Married: November 23, 1946

Los Angeles, California

Ray and Florence remain active in church activities. Although he's technically retired, Ray still enjoys the occasional odd job. Florence considers herself lucky to have a spouse who shares her active outlook on life.

⋇

What better partnership is there than that of a loving husband and wife striving together to achieve common objectives? And who better to join forces with than the one you love, the person with whom you've chosen to share your deepest hopes, your fondest dreams, your very life?

One of the biggest problems marriages face today is that spouses cling to their own individuality rather than fully entering into their new identity as a couple. They hold on to independence at the expense of the unity God intended, maintaining separate checkbooks, separate pursuits, separate vacations, separate friends. Oftentimes they unknowingly have different visions for their marriage and their future.

The Bible says, "Two people can accomplish more than twice as much as one; they get a better return for their labor. . . . A triple-braided cord is not easily broken" (Ecclesiastes 4:9, 12 NLT). Look closely at a length of rope; there is individuality still present in the strands, but it disappears into the oneness of the cord. What you hold in your hand is a single, strong rope powerful enough to move heavy loads.

God has designed marriage to make the two of you stronger together than you ever were when you were single. As a result, you don't need to be afraid to set big goals. Why don't you and your spouse talk today about what your life together was meant to accomplish?

This explains why a man leaves his father and mother and is joined to his wife, and the two are united into one.
Genesis 2:24 nlt

Always treat your wife like a lady.

Sol & Edna Weiss

Married: June 16, 1946

New York City, New York

Sol and Edna met at a party when he was fourteen
and she was thirteen. "We still hold hands," Sol says.
"And I still put up with his sense of humor," Edna laughs.

Showing a woman honor and respect involves so much more than chivalrous gestures such as holding a door, rising politely at the dinner table, or laying one's coat over a puddle of rainwater. A husband's treatment of his wife like a lady begins with his attitude toward her. Does he truly value his spouse, or does he take her for granted? Does he view her as a gift from heaven above or as more of a burden, "the ol' ball and chain"? The Bible describes a wife of noble character as "her husband's crown" (Proverbs 12:4), "worth far more than rubies" (Proverbs 31:10).

A godly wife is a treasure to be cherished, deserving her husband's highest compliments and praise.

Honoring his wife begins with his thoughts and feelings toward her, but it doesn't end there. Picture a valiant young knight striving to win his lady's affections, and revealing his heart to her through his words and deeds! He gives her his full attention when she is speaking. He considers her point of view. He respects her opinions and empathizes with her feelings. In addition, he regards the issues that concern her as important. And he celebrates her triumphs and commends her for her virtues.

God is calling wives to be true ladies, kindhearted and worthy of respect; He is calling husbands to be sincere gentlemen, and to give their wives the honor they have earned.

Husbands, . . . be considerate as you live with
your wives, and treat them with respect.

1 Peter 3:7

Part of having a happy marriage is developing similar interests.

Paul & Gean Young

Married: August 27, 1946

Marion, Ohio

Paul and Gean met at the Highway Rollerina. They enjoy traveling, boating, bike rides, and just being together outdoors.

❊

Friendship is such an integral part of romance. The joy of sharing experiences – sights, sounds, tastes, aromas, sensations – will abound as a husband and wife explore and revel in the delights of God's creation. Having fun and enjoying life together is one of the greatest benefits of married life, and it forms a tight bond that can cement a marriage through the years.

Whatever you do, don't neglect this important aspect of marriage. Whether it be traveling to an exotic locale, taking dance lessons, sampling unusual food at an ethnic restaurant, learning a new sport, doing volunteer work for a local charity, or trying some inexpensive activity that one or both of you have never done before, do it together! It will stimulate conversation, nurture your friendship, promote unity in your marriage, and keep your hearts aglow.

Spouses truly should be best friends. Developing common interests helps ensure that a couple will draw closer together over time rather than slowly drift apart. Best of all, it fosters an intimacy that goes far deeper than friendship, because it involves one of the chief ingredients of a happy, successful union – quality time shared together. In more than one sense, it takes a lot of time for a marriage to last forever.

What can you do today to begin building the friendship part of your relationship?

Come, dear lover – let's tramp through the countryside.
Let's sleep at some wayside inn, then rise early and listen
to   bird-song. Let's look for wildflowers in bloom, blackberry
bushes blossoming white, Fruit trees festooned with
cascading flowers.

Song of Songs 7:11-12 msg

Learn to bend and not break.

Gerald & Evelyn Smith

Married: May 2, 1946

Oklahoma City, Oklahoma

Gerald and Evelyn met soon after Gerald returned from World War II. Evelyn was renting a duplex from his parents, and Gerald came to fix the oven. "He just wouldn't leave, so I asked him to supper," says Evelyn. "He still wouldn't leave – so I married him."

※

Life's storms are capable of generating powerful winds. Business layoffs, family illnesses or injuries, financial crises, time pressures, breakdowns in close relationships, problems at work, misunderstandings at home – all these, and some windstorms far more devastating, threaten to snap a marriage in two and bring it crashing to the ground if a couple is unable to endure the gusts.

If your marriage is to survive, you must possess a kind of supple strength. Flexibility is an important component of this quality; however, the ability to bend under pressure does not come from abandoning principles and convictions. Rather, it comes from trusting God and submitting to His will for your lives. And true strength is found, not by drawing from some inner personal reserve nor by leaning too heavily on each other, but by sinking roots deeper and deeper into your trust in the promises of God, and together relying on Him to come through for you. A marriage thus secured will never be broken apart or uprooted.

Sometimes supple strength involves a willingness to adapt to change. It means letting go of circumstances you are trying to control and leaving the outcome to God. When the storm finally clears, the landscape around you may be drastically altered, but your marriage remains intact, standing firm, and continues to thrive in its new environment.

Are there places you need to bend in your marriage?

Blessed is the man who trusts in the LORD, whose confidence is in him. He will be like a tree planted by the water that sends out its roots by the stream. It does not fear when heat comes; its leaves are always green.

Jeremiah 17:7-8

Love always takes maintenance – kindness is a big part of that!

Merle & Evelyn Lashey

Married: December 20, 1946

Marion, Ohio

Merle and Evelyn well remember the moment they first saw each other.
Merle was a basketball player, Evelyn a cheerleader for the rival school.
Their eyes met, and needless to say, Merle played a great game that night!

※

Home maintenance requires a great deal of money, time, and effort.
A broken shingle must be replaced, a torn screen mended, a squeaky
hinge oiled, a leaky tap fixed. Yet how pleasant it is to live in a house
where the roof keeps out the rain, the windows keep out the bugs, the
doors swing freely – and ne'er the sound of a dripping faucet is heard!

While "love maintenance" may not require as much money, it does take a lot of time and effort, and, of course, kindness. Make a careful inspection of your marriage. Observe the interactions within your home, and then compile a "to do" list (and a "not to do list"). Pay special attention to the little things, which make such a big difference in a relationship.

Do you become exasperated when asked to repeat something? Has sarcasm crept into your vocabulary? Are you harboring a "Do it yourself" attitude instead of a servant's heart? Must you always prove you're right? Do you often say, "I told you so"? Do you fix blame every time something goes wrong? Do you maximize your spouse's mistakes?

The Bible says (twice!), "A quarrelsome wife is like a constant dripping" (Proverbs 19:13). It's a warning husbands should heed as well. Get busy on those lists and discover how enjoyable and long-lasting a well-maintained marriage can be.

Be kind to one another, tenderhearted.

Ephesians 4:32 nkjv

Do everything together.

Robert & Bette Barto
Married: July 18, 1946
Chicago, Illinois

Robert and Bette are seldom apart and remain very active socially.
They're also proud that for more than fifty years,
they've spent every Christmas Eve with their sons.

☀

Families today are pulled apart in so many ways. Busyness keeps everyone on the run, with little time to share a meal or a meaningful conversation. Televisions, computers, video games, and CD players isolate family members within the home; and work, school, sports, and a myriad of entertainment options separate them without.

A husband and wife must intentionally make time to spend together as a couple, and time for everyone to interact as a family. This doesn't preclude the above activities; doing together is more rewarding than just being together! The secret is to resist the pull toward disconnection.

If one family member is involved in a sport, have everyone else attend the games regularly to shout encouragement. Hide the headphones of the CD player and turn on the speakers; take turns playing DJ, and have a dance contest! Host a video game tournament including everyone's favorite games, with a handicap system so anyone can win. If it's just the two of you, try finding a hobby, volunteer activity, or church ministry in which both of you can become involved.

Pray about this. It may take some creativity and effort in today's individualistic culture, but with God's help you can keep your marriage and family intact. After all, His promise in Psalm 128 includes the blessing of togetherness.

Your wife will be like a fruitful vine within your house;
Your sons will be like olive shoots around your table.
Thus is the man blessed who fears the LORD.

Psalm 128:3-4

Don't expect to have everything right at the start.

M. L. "Dutch" & Lula Mae Noah

Married: March 27, 1946

Centerton, Arkansas

Dutch and Lula Mae believe a good marriage grows over time. "Dutch was a milk-hauler for forty-one years," says Lula Mae. "We didn't have much at first, but we had each other." Dutch adds, "Marriage, children, grandchildren–what more could a man want from life?"

A young couple gets married and immediately begins to accumulate large amounts of debt trying to establish and maintain the lifestyle of their parents, without considering that their folks have worked hard for years to earn their possessions. The couple sails along smoothly for a few years, but then an unexpected event thrusts them into financial difficulty, which causes much stress and threatens to destroy their marriage.

The Bible urges, "Keep your lives free from the love of money and be content with what you have, because God has said, 'Never will I leave you; never will I forsake you'" (Hebrews 13:5). What a promise! And what more reason for contentment is needed than to be married to one's beloved and to know that the God of the universe is ever present, watching over, guiding, providing, protecting?

Paul claimed to have learned the secret of contentment. Whatever else this secret may entail, surely it involves a constant awareness of God's goodness and His presence. Such awareness can be fostered by daily Bible reading, spending time talking and listening to God, and spending regular time with people who know God well. Try it. You will be rewarded with more than contentment; you will have God's friendship too!

Godliness with contentment is great gain.

1 Timothy 6:6

Everyone has problems – just stay together and work them out!

John & Clarice Gillespie

Married: March 5, 1945

Phoenix, Arizona

Since John was in the army when he and Clarice met, Clarice had to work.
When John got out, she continued working to put him through school.
"Our long marriage is just good economics," quips Clarice.
"I had to stick around to get my money's worth!"

⁂

God wants to ensure a couple is not alone in their marriage – He wants to be an integral part of their union. He is always present, always available, always ready to help the pair through any difficulty if they will follow His commands.

Inevitably, trouble comes. Often a disagreement will break out, tempers will flare, and soon an impenetrable wall has risen between you.

Communication has broken down, leading to isolation, frustration, and despair.

At times like these it's a blessing to know that you have access to a God who is all-wise, all-powerful, and always willing to listen. When you can't talk to your spouse, talk to the Lord. Ask Him to help resolve the situation.

God has unlimited perspective; He can see over the wall. He perceives with utter clarity and can lay bare the root of the problem. Sometimes it is a simple misunderstanding. Sometimes God will provide one of you with insight into the other's deeply felt but unexpressed needs. In any case, God will reveal to each of you your share of the blame and prompt you to humbly seek forgiveness, leading to reconciliation and unity. Then you can rejoice, saying, "He tore down the wall" (Ephesians 2:14 MSG).

Make God a partner in your marriage today, and He will make your marriage strong for all your tomorrows.

I look up to the mountains – does my help
come from there? My help comes from the LORD,
who made the heavens and the earth!

Psalm 121:1-2 nlt

Always be best friends with your partner.

Lowell & Lorraine Barber

Married: October 23, 1945

Two Buttes, Colorado

Lowell and Lorraine have a knack for keeping friendships in the family. "Two of my good friends married two of his brothers," Lorraine says proudly. Lowell raises exotic chickens, while Lorraine likes to cook – but not his chickens! "That's not allowed," she laughs.

What is a best friend?

Someone to be there? Acquaintances, even close friends and family members, will walk with you awhile along life's road and then depart, but Proverbs 18:24 says, "A real friend sticks closer than a brother" (NLT). In your spouse, God has blessed you with a friend for life, a traveling companion who will share both panoramic vistas and difficult terrain – and one day celebrate with you the journey's end.

Someone to offer a hand? Ecclesiastes 4:10 says, "If one person falls, the other can reach out and help" (NLT). Your truest friend is the one who offers assistance when you've stumbled into the roadside ditch. A loving spouse will pull you up, affirm your worth, and encourage you to strive ahead.

Someone to talk to? "The pleasantness of one's friend springs from his earnest counsel" (Proverbs 27:9). Your best friend is the one you want to be with most, the one you choose to talk to first whether the road is smooth or rough, the one with whom you want to share your thoughts and feelings, the one whose opinion and advice you seek.

A best friend is all these. But mostly, according to Proverbs 17:17, it is someone who cares deeply: "A friend loves at all times" (NIV). May your best friend always be your spouse.

This is my lover, this my friend.
Song of Songs 5:16

Really get to know each other *before* you marry.

Howard & Barbara Rampton

Married: December 20, 1945

Sydney, Australia

Howard and Barbara did most of their courting long distance. "She was in Sydney and I was working in Victoria – six hundred miles away!" Howard says. Since their marriage, they've enjoyed traveling to many different places, including Spain, Tahiti, Scandinavia, Singapore, and England.

Courtship is a time of discovery, a time for gaining insight into another person's character, for evaluating their potential as a marriage partner. The understanding gleaned from this time of acquaintance helps a couple determine whether they have the "right stuff" for building a life-long relationship.

The book of Ruth in the Bible describes the courtship between Boaz, a wealthy landowner, and Ruth, a poor widow whom he discovers in his field, gathering leftover grain. Before they married, they learned of each other's reputation, experienced one another's kindness, and received advice from other people.

Boaz told Ruth, "All my fellow townsmen know that you are a woman of noble character" (Ruth 3:11); Ruth knew that Boaz was "a man of standing" (Ruth 2:1). Upon experiencing Ruth's goodness, Boaz said, "This kindness is greater than that which you showed earlier: You have not run after the younger men" (Ruth 3:10). Likewise, Ruth told him, "You have given me comfort and have spoken kindly" (Ruth 2:13). Naomi commended Boaz to Ruth repeatedly, and Boaz received the blessing of the town's elders.

Ruth shows us an ancient truth that still works today: Take the time and make the effort to truly get to know one another before marriage. The character of each spouse frames the home which, when built upon the foundation of God's love, makes it stable.

A house is built by wisdom and becomes strong through good sense. Through knowledge its rooms are filled with all sorts of precious riches and valuables.

Proverbs 24:3-4 nlt

If you speak in haste, apologize with haste, too!

Bill & June Vogt

Married: March 30, 1944

Takoma Park, Maryland

*Bill and June met in college. "He asked me for a date as
I was coming out of class," June remembers. She adds that they
have been friends from the very beginning of their relationship.
Today they enjoy landscaping and reading together.*

Harmful words come so quickly! Emotions rise, and before the
rational mind can intercede, haste causes the tongue to lash out angrily,
wounding the person most dear to you. You feel regret, but then pride
prevents you from speaking words of apology, words that soothe hurt
feelings and restore your relationship.

You have two enemies to contend with: haste and pride. If you lose the fight with the first, you must win the battle with the second, or the war may be lost.

In the initial skirmish, remember that it is okay to feel angry, but it is never okay to sin. Anger is a human emotion that everyone experiences; even our Lord Jesus grew angry. However, Jesus showed us that it is possible to be angry yet not engage in hasty, sinful behavior.

If haste defeats you, and you find you have sinned by saying something you shouldn't have, subdue your pride and apologize. A wise man said, "Pride goes before destruction, and haughtiness before a fall" (Proverbs 16:18 NLT). In the short term, pride brings a temporary breakdown in your relationship; unchecked, it could result in the collapse of the marriage.

Save your marriage. Dispense with pride by humbling yourself and offering a heartfelt apology – posthaste!

Rash language cuts and maims;
but there is healing in the words of the wise.
Proverbs 12:18 msg

Heartwarmers

Take a quiet walk
together in the woods.

Have a picnic breakfast
in the backyard.

Cuddle up in a hammock
in the shade.

Always be honest, faithful, and true to each other.

Ralph & Hilda Standverry

Married: December 27, 1944

Rabun County, Georgia

Ralph and Hilda grew up in the same "holler" in North Carolina. "He used to think I was a nuisance when we were five, but not anymore," Hilda says with a grin.

☀

Marriage is the greatest, most intimate opportunity you will have in your lifetime to minister to another person. Only you can't do it on your own. To make the most of this opportunity, we must look to Jesus to both teach us and make us able to love each other.

We begin by learning more about Jesus and striving to emulate His perfect love. However, we can only love successfully by asking Him to change us. The secret of the Christian life is that Jesus Himself turns us into new people – the loving kind.

This is what the Bible means when Colossians 3:9-10 says, "Do not lie to each other, since you have taken off your old self with its practices and have put on the new self, which is being renewed in knowledge in the image of its Creator."

And there is no better way to bless your spouse than to ask God to make you the kind of person who remains true to your vows and faithful to your promises.

Spend some time talking to Him about teaching you to love and making you more like Jesus today. You'll be glad you did – and so will your spouse.

I saw heaven standing open and there before me was a white horse, whose rider is called Faithful and True.

Revelation 19:11

Remember, the Golden Rule also applies to your spouse.

Gerald & Geneva Clark

Married: October 27, 1944

Spartanburg, South Carolina

Gerald and Geneva grew up a mountain apart. Twice a week for five years,
Gerald walked fourteen miles between mountains to "court" Geneva.
"I was afraid if I wasn't persistent, someone else would get her,"
he says. They enjoy reading and taking walks together.

※

What is the extent of your duty as husband or wife?

Jesus once said, "'You must love the Lord your God with all your heart, all your soul, and all your mind.' This is the first and greatest commandment. A second is equally important: 'Love your neighbor as yourself.' All the other commandments and all the demands of the prophets are based on these two commandments" (Matthew 22:37-40 NLT).

46

When He spoke about all the other commandments and demands, Jesus meant the whole of God's Word, the Old Testament Bible. Thus he was saying that the entire scope of our duty as God's people can be summed up in one word – *love*.

"Who is my neighbor?" Jesus was asked on another occasion (Luke 10:29 NLT). If, as a married person, you were to ask Him this question, He would tell you that you have many neighbors, the closest of whom is your mate.

Be the best of neighbors to your spouse! Treat your partner exactly as you want to be treated – with honor, respect, gratitude, gentleness, civility, patience, kindness, humility, politeness, thoughtfulness, forgiveness. God's command to you, His desire for you, can be summed up, once again, in one word.

Do for others what you would like them to do for you.

Matthew 7:12 nlt

Never consider getting "unmarried" as an option.

Art & Angie Grumbine

Married: February 5, 1944

Tujunga, California

Art and Angie have thirteen children.

Early in their marriage, if not before the wedding, a couple should look each other in the eye and solemnly agree, "Divorce is not an option." If both spouses own this commitment, if they truly lock that door once and for all, they will have made tremendous progress in building a marriage to last a lifetime.

The benefits of such a commitment are immediate: both partners experience a sense of security, a sense that their hearts are protected, that the relationship can be trusted and there is hope for the future. Over time, each spouse will feel free to spend mental and emotional energy focusing on problem solving rather than worrying about being abandoned, or entertaining notions of escape. And the end result is a satisfying lifelong union!

The Lord will honor your commitment, because you are aligning your will squarely with His. He will help you keep it – through prayer, through His Word, through the counsel of godly people, and through His personal help – offering guidance and wisdom far beyond your own. And He will bless you for your faithfulness. The Bible says, "You need to persevere so that when you have done the will of God, you will receive what he has promised" (Hebrews 10:36). God will surely see that you both get the reward you have earned.

What about you? Have you committed yourself to marriage for life? Let your spouse know.

[Love] always protects, always trusts,
always hopes, always perseveres.
1 Corinthians 13:7

Share responsibility. She was boss the first fifty years – I've got the next fifty!

Lawrence & Glenyce Jensen

Married: September 23, 1944

Sac City, Iowa

Lawrence and Glenyce first met when he offered her a ride on a Harley he was taking care of for his brother, who was in the military. For their honeymoon, they drove forty-three miles to Fort Dodge – in spite of gas rationing and a strictly enforced thirty-five-mile-per-hour speed limit!

֍

If you and your beloved have ever both tried being in charge when working on a project together (especially one in which neither partner has any real expertise), you know how frustrating it can be! There's no better formula for fruitless arguments over how to get the job done, and bitter I-told-you-so's when things go awry.

A much better plan – modeled for us in the Garden of Eden – is to assign one partner authority and responsibility, while the other serves as a helper. Now, the helper is free to offer suggestions and advice, but the leader is the one who decides which course of action to take. The helper must agree to abide by the leader's decisions. In this way, the work can progress, with both partners laboring together in harmony. And if something does go wrong, it's the leader's responsibility – with input from the helper, but no reprehensions – to determine how to make it right.

The next time a task presents itself, pull out a captain's hat (real or imaginary), draw straws, cast lots, or find some other way to figure out who should wear it this time, and hand the other person a first-mate's cap. Or simply say to your spouse, "Okay, today I'm Gilligan, and you're the Skipper!"

GOD said, "It's not good for the Man to be alone;
I'll make him a helper, a companion."

Genesis 2:18 msg

Give each other plenty of space to grow.

David & Mildred Garner

Married: June 11, 1944

National City, California

David met Mildred when she was an aircraft riveter and he was a marine. "It takes a lot of grit and grace to keep a marriage together," laughs Mildred. The Garners raised seven children and are proud of their family – especially their twenty great-grandchildren!

※

You love your spouse, so naturally you want to see them realize their full potential – physically, intellectually, emotionally, and most importantly, spiritually. We are called to "grow in the special favor and knowledge of our Lord and Savior Jesus Christ" (2 Peter 3:18 NLT). God wants us to become mature, especially in our ability to trust Him and follow His instructions. Therefore you must give each other room to grow.

This may mean encouraging your partner to enroll in a college course, volunteer with a nonprofit organization, join a book club, or take a Sunday school class. It may involve self-sacrifice as you relinquish your mate's attention so they can pursue these activities.

Sometimes it also means giving your spouse room to suffer. Husbands, particularly, can be overprotective, trying to shield their wives from situations that, although painful, bring about meaningful growth in character. James 1:3-4 says, "For when your faith is tested, your endurance has a chance to grow. So let it grow, for when your endurance is fully developed, you will be strong in character and ready for anything" (NLT).

Open your arms and release your beloved into the arms of the Lord, who has promised to work all things out for our good. Seek ways to encourage your spouse's growth.

God, who began the good work within you, will continue his work until it is finally finished on that day when Christ Jesus comes back again.

Philippians 1:6 nlt

Agree that it's okay to disagree.

Bill & Rachel Bergherm

Married: April 6, 1944

Takoma Park, Maryland

Bill and Rachel met in the kitchen of the hospital where they were working their way through college. Today they enjoy traveling to third-world countries to help build churches and schools.

∗⁄∗

"They had such a sharp disagreement that they parted company."

This statement from Acts 15:39 refers to the apostle Paul and Barnabas, who were arguing about whether to bring Mark along on their next journey. Yet it could also serve as an epitaph for so many relationships!

If you and your spouse plan to remain travel partners for life, you must find ways to prevent simple differences of opinion from escalating into verbal warfare powerful enough to send you on your separate ways. It's imperative that you learn to "fight fair" when disagreements arise.

Mainly, fighting fair involves keeping the discussion – lively as it may be – focused on the issue at hand, not dredging up past grievances; attacking the problem, not the person; and maintaining an open-mindedness and willingness to listen. Foremost on the agenda must be affirming the relationship, reassuring each other by your words, tone, and body language that even though you don't share the same opinion, you love, value, and respect each other.

Invite God into your debates. He's a great referee, and He will eventually lead you to unity. He might bring one of you a fresh insight, convince one of you to submit to the other, or perhaps direct you both to a compromise solution. In the meantime, be thankful that the Lord made each of you unique!

Put up with each other.

Colossians 3:13 cev

When you get into an argument, take a good long walk to cool down.

Melvin & Margaret Elliston

Married: June 12, 1944

Takoma Park, Maryland

Melvin and Margaret met in a college art class. "The truth is, I came to college to get a degree, and she came to college to get me," Melvin laughs. Both love sharing the vegetables and flowers on their North Carolina farm. "He plants them, and I pick them," Margaret adds.

⁂

Some people think it's always better to express feelings than to repress them. But in the heat of an argument, emotions arise that often are better left unspoken, for thoughtless words can cause frightful damage to a loved one's heart and soul. And a wound inflicted in an instant may take months to heal.

So call a time-out. Gently suggest, "Let's cool off a bit and talk about this later." Then get alone and take a long walk. Draw a hot bath or take a brisk shower. Go for a leisurely drive. Ride a bike. Read a book or listen to some music. Spend some time in prayer.

Exercise will burn off steam, clear your head, and improve your mood. A book or music might take your mind off things for a while. A bath or shower could help you relax. And time with the Lord – which could flow from any other activity – will certainly bring refreshment, renewal, and perspective.

Ephesians 4:26 says, "Do not let the sun go down while you are still angry." So if you take a long walk, be sure to turn around eventually and walk back to your spouse! The Bible doesn't say you have to resolve every issue by sundown – simply leave your anger behind when you return home. There'll be time for problem solving tomorrow.

A fool gives full vent to his anger,
but a wise man keeps himself under control.
Proverbs 29:11

Talk things out and never give up!

Delbert & Wanda Wilkins

Married: January 9, 1943

Lawton, Oklahoma

Delbert and Wanda have had a busy life with eight children and a successful business.

※

Each spouse carries a unique load of emotional baggage into a marriage. All of us, to a greater or lesser extent, bear painful memories and relational scars from our formative years. This baggage can cause communication problems between a husband and wife.

Often, a person will hear a message vastly different from what their spouse intended to convey. "You forgot to put your glass in the dishwasher" can be interpreted as "You're a lazy slob and a failure." A safety reminder from a concerned father can sound to his wife like, "You're a horrible mother! I don't trust you with our child."

Sounds like an overreaction, doesn't it? And of course it is. But these misunderstandings are common and lead to much conflict in marriages.

Choosing words carefully can help you avoid some of them. But misunderstandings are sure to come, and when they do, the best way to deal with them is to keep communicating. When you sense that your mate is upset by something you said, don't allow the anger to fester for a moment. Clarify your statement and ask questions to ensure you are understood properly. Reassure your partner of your love and respect.

Never give up trying to express your feelings; never give up trying to understand your spouse. Communication can be hard work, but the rewards are worth it.

Don't get tired of doing what is good.
Don't get discouraged and give up, for we will reap
a harvest of blessing at the appropriate time.
Galatians 6:9 nlt

Marriage is not fifty-fifty – you both have to be willing to give more.

Ray & Gloria Ferry

Married: February 28, 1943

Las Vegas, Nevada

Ray and Gloria operated a successful business together, allowing them to spend far more time with each other than do most couples. In addition to their other activities, they still take time to play golf together at least twice each week.

꙳

We are called by God to lovingly serve one another. Being married gives you the chance to serve another person every day, in ways both large and small.

Don't just give 50 percent, being content to pull your half of the load and worrying about whether your partner is pulling their half; give 100 percent of your effort. If you ask, God will provide you with the energy you'll need. When you see something that needs to be done, don't think about whose job it is – simply do it. And don't seek accolades or gratitude or favors in return.

Our actions and attitude should be like Jesus'. He was willing to serve others, to the point of washing their feet. This was how He expressed His deep love. Jesus has invited us to follow His example and minister to the needs of those around us. So serve one another humbly and willingly. Let your actions flow from the love in your heart.

Whatever you do, don't keep score. Marriage is not a contest in which you and your spouse are pitted against one another. Rather, God has placed you on the same team so you can strive together toward victory.

Remember, when it comes to serving each other, be loving; go the extra mile.

Serve each other with love.

Galatians 5:13 cev

If your spouse gets bossy, just stay sweet.

Willard & Estelle Church

Married: December 7, 1943

Houston, Texas

Willard and Estelle were born in the same town and met in the fourth grade. Willard served as a medic in the Philippines and Korea, later building homes and operating a broom-making business. Estelle spent twenty-five years working in a bakery.

A five-year-old offers a toy to his younger sister; she giggles and hands him a crayon. Later he sticks out his tongue, and she responds with a loud raspberry.

Attitude is contagious!

It's amazing how much influence you and your spouse have over each other. You can be breezing along, humming a tune, having a wonderful day; but when your mate drifts by like a little dark cloud, scowling and blocking the sun, notice how quickly your sky turns gray.

You now have a choice. You can allow yourself to be dragged down into a sullen disposition and provoked into an argument, or you can smile, speak kindly, and spread some sunshine of your own. You might be surprised to see that little dark cloud turn all white and fluffy!

God calls us to shine light where there is darkness, to respond to bad with good. When your spouse is irritable and treats you poorly, you don't have to reciprocate. There's a better choice. To the immature, the Golden Rule seems to be, "Do to others as they have done to you." But we know that unkind treatment is a childish, knee-jerk response, and we are instead called to thoughtful, mature behavior.

What can you do today to shed light in your marriage?

Gracious speech is like clover honey –
good taste to the soul, quick energy for the body.
Proverbs 16:24 msg

Watch how a prospective spouse's family treats one another.

Clifford & Carol Clark

Married: July 14, 1943

Stone, Saskatchewan, Canada

Clifford met Carol when he took eggs from his farm to sell to her mother. His visits continued, and eventually he wound up with more than egg money! The couple are now retired from farming and cattle ranching but still enjoy helping out on their son's wheat farm.

⋇

There is a blessing that flows from generation to generation of those who love, honor, and obey God. Psalm 103:17 proclaims, "From everlasting to everlasting the LORD's love is with those who fear him, and his righteousness with their children's children."

When you marry into a family who truly love God and each other, you receive the benefits of this generational blessing. It's a rich spiritual inheritance which you and your spouse will enjoy and then have the privilege to pass along to your children, your grandchildren, and beyond.

Observe how the family members of your sweetheart behave toward each other. Do they treat each other with respect? Is Christlike love displayed in their lives? When they disagree, do they take off the gloves and fight unfairly, or do they keep their composure and calmly work out their differences? If a crisis arises, bringing pressure and stress upon the family members, do they pull apart and begin to point fingers at each other, or do they draw together, look heavenward for help, and offer one another comfort, encouragement, and support?

A spouse from a godly family will bring the blessing they have received to your marriage. And better yet, you and your spouse can also bestow this blessing upon your children by being godly.

I have never seen the righteous forsaken or their children begging bread. They are always generous and lend freely; their children will be blessed.

Psalm 37:25-26

You can do everything together – even shopping!

Bill & Ruthe Ambler

Married: June 27, 1943

Utica, New York

Bill and Ruthe first caught each other's eye in a college woodworking class. "We started with very little, living in a tent while we worked at revival meetings," Ruthe remembers. They've now retired to a lovely mountain home and enjoy browsing local flea markets.

✲

Life can get so busy that you find you and your spouse feel more like alienated college roommates than a married couple. How can you get quality time together? Sometimes doing the simple things you have to do anyway can provide opportunities to spend time with your favorite person. Why not get groceries together? You can talk as you stroll through the aisles and fill the basket. You can make dinner preparation or cleanup a very special time as well. Doing the simple things of life together can keep you both in tune with each other because you have regular opportunities to talk over things while you get done what has to be done anyway.

Go one step further and find fun things to do that you can both enjoy. If your spouse is enjoying a book, read it after they finish and have a special coffee shop meeting to discuss it. If one of you has a penchant for woodworking, the other one can make a twosome out of lumber store visits. And just sitting in the shop and talking while your spouse works can be a way of enjoying time together.

Take some time and look at your schedule. Think about the things that have to be done each day and find ways of sharing those tasks together.

My goal is that they will be encouraged and knit together by strong ties of love.

Colossians 2:2 nlt

Learn to be unselfish. Always put the other's interests first.

Claude & Elizabeth Steen

Married: March 25, 1943

Alahambra, California

*Claude and Elizabeth met at an all-girls summer camp where he
was helping his mother. "I wrote in Elizabeth's autograph book,
'Hope I get to know you better someday.' And I certainly did!"*

It's healthy for a married man or woman to pursue personal interests and engage in individual activities. This provides an outlet, a sense
of freedom, perhaps some exercise, and interaction with others – plus,
it makes for a more interesting, well-rounded spouse, which keeps the
conversation at home lively! However, the level of your involvement in
these pursuits must be weighed carefully against the effect it will have on
your marriage.

You must consider your partner's needs as well as your own. Time is a precious and limited resource that God has given you as a couple. Your mate has a large stake in any decision you make concerning how you will spend your hours, because every choice has important ramifications for you both. Not only can too much time apart erode the unity of your marriage, it can deprive your spouse of legitimate needs such as time together, help around the house, or a break from the kids.

So be generous. Think of your spouse's interests before chasing yours. Involve your partner in analyzing the pros and cons of your commitment to any activity. Sure, your relationship may benefit if you regularly enjoy some time to yourself; just don't forget to count the costs. And make sure your mate gets equal personal time!

Let each of you look out not only for his own interests,
but also for the interests of others.

Philippians 2:4 nkjv

Never go to sleep at night without saying, "I love you" – and meaning it!

Robert & Rachel Stewart

Married: June 14, 1943

Atlanta, Georgia

Robert and Rachel met at his brother's wedding. "It was love at first sight for me," Robert says with a grin, "but Rachel took a little convincing."

⁓

As husband and wife, you have a wonderful chance to connect with each other meaningfully every night as you retire for the evening, if you take the opportunity to embrace one another and speak tender words of affection. It's such a comfort and a joy to drift asleep wrapped in the arms of your beloved, with the words "I love you" echoing in your ear. You not only sense your spouse's love, you can almost feel God's touch and hear

His voice! It's a gentle reminder that He is always watching over you, even as you sleep.

Sadly, night after night many couples climb into bed, say a curt "Good night, dear," roll over, and miss their chance to connect so intimately and bless one another so richly. It's not that they're upset or angry; they've simply begun to take each other, and the time together God has so graciously given them, for granted.

Don't make that mistake. Cuddle up at night, even if only for a moment, and give your spouse that marvelous physical, emotional, and spiritual sensation of warmth, comfort, belonging, and security. And as you whisper words of love, remember: "Love must be sincere" (Romans 12:9). So prove your love with deeds by day, then express it once more at night – speaking from your heart.

He who watches over you will not slumber; indeed,
he who watches over Israel will neither slumber nor sleep.

Psalm 121:3-4

You have to like each other – not just be able to talk, but really communicate!

Sam & Mae Richiusa

Married: May 23, 1942

Yuma, Arizona

Sam and Mae are both children of Italian immigrants. They fell in love when they were very young, and eloped as soon as they were old enough.

❊

Your marriage is affected by the quality of each of your individual relationships with God. Blessings come to you as a result of your faithfulness to Him. As 1 John 1:7 promises, "If we walk in the light, God himself being the light, we also experience a shared life with one another" (MSG).

Your primary responsibility is to keep God's commandments and live in a manner pleasing to Him, emulating Jesus in your attitudes and behavior. God changes you and your spouse into loving people as you both spend time with Him, and you then begin to relate to your spouse in a way that encourages closeness, unity, affection, and love.

For example, you become the kind of person who speaks truthfully, but always in a way that is gracious and loving. Your language does not come across as unwholesome or demeaning, but rather it encourages your partner and builds them up. Perhaps most importantly, you are never afraid to express your love, using words that are all the more powerful because they are supported by your actions. In short, you speak as Jesus spoke, and He really knew how to communicate.

First, nurture your relationship with God through Bible reading, prayer, and obedience. Let God bring His blessing upon your marriage by letting Him teach you loving ways to communicate with your spouse.

Try your best to let God's Spirit keep your hearts united.

Ephesians 4:3 cev

Always be totally honest and open with each other.

Paul & Georgia Bateman

Married: March 14, 1942

Anadarko, Oklahoma

Paul and Georgia did a lot of talking before they were married and have never stopped. "Doesn't matter if it's big or small," says Georgia. "We talk over everything." When Paul returned from World War II (with four bronze stars), they bought a farm and began a small dairy.

⁂

Every person has a deep need for intimacy, to know and be known by another human being. The first man, Adam, felt this need even in the Garden of Eden as he gazed at the wide variety of animals and realized there was no one like him. Then God gave Adam a wife to be his loving companion.

At first there were no secrets in Paradise. "Although Adam and his wife were both naked, neither of them felt any shame" (Genesis 2:25 NLT).

Adam and Eve enjoyed perfect intimacy, both physically and emotionally. But after they disobeyed God, they felt the need to hide – from God and each other. Wrongdoing was the enemy of intimacy and trust.

When you think about it, why would you want to hold anything back from your spouse or deceive your beloved in any way? You might gain some short-term peace. Yet there is so much to lose in the long run.

True intimacy begins by being completely honest with God. After all, He knows you better than anyone, even yourself. Confess your shortcomings to the Lord and receive His forgiveness and acceptance. He'll give you the power to change too.

Come out of hiding. You will no longer feel the need for even the smallest deception. Best of all, the intimacy you long for – with God and with each other – will grow.

An honest answer is like a warm hug.

Proverbs 24:26 msg

Keep your love, your health, and your faith in God strong.

Robert & Gladys Patterson

Married: June 14, 1942

Liberal, Kansas

Robert and Gladys met when he worked on a harvest crew. "I came in mostly asleep after running the combine all night," Robert laughs, "and Gladys gave me a cup of coffee – with a teaspoon of salt in it!" "I don't know what got into me," Gladys says, "but at least he noticed me!"

It takes work to keep the flames of romance burning brightly. Kind words, helpful deeds, a listening ear, the willingness to share, thoughtful little gifts, time together – all are like logs to be placed on the fire, carefully, tenderly, at just the right time and in just the right way. A fire requires skillful stoking, or it will slowly die.

In the same way, our bodies need attention. We must eat right, get plenty of rest, exercise regularly, practice safety, seek proper healthcare, and avoid harmful substances. Taking commonsense measures to stay healthy is a precious gift we can give ourselves and our spouse. It's also a way to thank God for the bodies He gave us.

To remain steadfast, marriage and health demand our effort – is it any different with our faith in God? The Bible speaks of our need to be encouraged, built up, and strengthened in our faith. We must work out spiritually to keep our faith in shape. The benefits of spiritual aerobics are far more valuable than those of physical exertion, because while the results of physical training affect us only during our lifetime, we can enjoy the benefits of spiritual training both today and throughout eternity.

It's important to exercise your body. It's important to exercise your heart and nurture your love. But it's even more important to exercise your faith.

Train yourself to be godly. For physical training is of some value, but godliness has value for all things, holding promise for both the present life and the life to come.

1 Timothy 4:7-8

Cooperation is the most important thing in a marriage.

Milton & Catherine Ewald

Married: November 25, 1942

Warwick, Rhode Island

Milton and Catherine are active seniors. Milton bikes, and Catherine swims. "When you get upset, just don't talk at all," Milton joked. "Eventually, you'll get lonesome and forget what you were fighting about!"

Marriage is a partnership. Partners work together to achieve a common objective, for their mutual benefit. The Bible describes such a relationship as being yoked together. When two oxen are teamed up, they must cooperate, or nothing will be accomplished. If the animals pull in different directions, the plow will have no effect.

The same is true of the marriage partnership. Are you and your spouse straining harmoniously toward a common goal? Or are you moving in opposite directions, bickering and fighting as you strive for separate visions of your future? Have you identified God's purpose for you as a married couple, and are you both working hard and making sacrifices to fulfill that purpose?

Oxen do not naturally work together; they need a leader, someone to guide them. Jesus said, "Take the yoke I give you. Put it on your shoulders and learn from me. . . . This yoke is easy to bear, and this burden is light" (Matthew 11:29-30 CEV). If you allow Him to, Jesus will provide the leadership you and your spouse need to cooperate successfully, giving you purpose, direction, and strength.

Though you cannot see Jesus walking before you, His Spirit is present nonetheless; and if you listen carefully – as you pray, as you read the Bible, as you're counseled by other believers – you will hear His voice clearly enough to follow.

Since we live by the Spirit, let us keep in step with the Spirit. Let us not become conceited, provoking and envying each other.

Galatians 5:25-26

Realize that neither of you is perfect.

John & Ida Mae Freeman

Married: November 17, 1942

Kissimmee, Florida

John and Ida Mae met on a double date. "She was with the other fella," John says, laughing. They enjoy traveling around the country in their motor home, especially to visit their ten grandchildren.

"Nobody's perfect."

Sometimes common sayings are rooted in eternal truth. God's Word agrees wholeheartedly with this one! The Bible says, "There is none righteous, no, not one" (Romans 3:10 NKJV). We've all made mistakes, we've all done wrong, and we've all fallen short of God's standard of perfection. God is the only one who is righteous, perfect, and good.

Both marriage partners are flawed, sinful people. No matter how hard we try to make our marriage perfect, we will have to deal with personal failings and hurt feelings. Unless we want to carry around a lot of anger and resentment for the rest of our lives, we will want to learn the best way to handle these situations. This is a hard truth.

But there is good news: God's way works. He has chosen to handle failure according to His good nature, which is gracious, patient, merciful, compassionate, and loving. Although He is greatly offended by wrong-doing, He immediately and freely pardons anyone who asks for forgiveness. And He never recalls it again.

Perhaps this is where we get the saying, "Forgive and forget."

If marriage partners, imperfect as they are, desire to build a good, lasting marriage, they will want to remember two things about love: It is slow to become angry, and it holds no memory of grievances.

Be gentle with one another, sensitive. Forgive one another as quickly and thoroughly as God in Christ forgave you.
Ephesians 4:32 msg

Find interests you can enjoy together.

Wharton & Corda Jane Sanders

Married: July 4, 1942

Hyattsville, Maryland

Wharton and Corda Jane discovered each other at a bus stop when he rescued her from a group of drunken sailors. "I usually didn't give out my phone number, but I made an exception in his case," she says with a smile.

✷

Having trouble finding something the two of you can do together?

The Bible suggests many activities that would be very pleasing to God. If you take any one of these ideas separately, think about it awhile, talk it over, and ask the Lord to show you how you could go about implementing it, you may discover a pursuit that both of you not only enjoy but also find deeply fulfilling.

Here are some of the activities that matter greatly to God: righting injustice, helping the oppressed, sharing the gospel, comforting the brokenhearted, freeing the captives, looking after widows, caring for orphans, feeding the hungry, providing drink to the thirsty, showing hospitality to strangers, clothing the naked, tending to the sick, visiting the prisoners.

This list could be a map that leads you in any number of directions. For example, ask yourselves, *Is there someone we know, someone in our community, or someone in another part of the world who is being held captive?* What about a young man addicted to alcohol? A single parent weighed down with too much responsibility? A family struggling with too much debt? Can you see the possibilities for involvement? Can you imagine the excitement of working side by side to meet others' needs, all the while serving God in the process?

What better way to spend your time?

Work for justice. Help the down-and-out.
Stand up for the homeless. Go to bat for the defenseless.
Isaiah 1:17 msg

Agree to walk away when a discussion becomes too heated.

Ralph & Marion Austin

Married: December 24, 1942

Kansas City, Kansas

Ralph and Marion were married during World War II.
Ralph served in the air force and survived thirty-five combat missions.
Today they enjoy watching and feeding the birds together.
Ralph grows a vegetable garden, Marion a flower garden.

All of us have said things we regret. In the midst of an argument, it's easy to let fly words we later wish we'd never spoken. Their effect is immediate: a wounded expression, a flood of increased anger, a response of more hurtful words, an escalation in the warfare.

When tempers flare, it is often best to postpone the discussion and spend some time apart. Get alone so you can calm down and collect your thoughts. Find someplace quiet and listen for the still, small voice of God.

He will speak to you both individually if you will give Him the opportunity, and He will direct you toward reconciliation.

Something within us wants to throw fuel on the fire during a disagreement. We can trace that urge back to our sinful nature. However, for the sake of your marriage and your spouse, you must control yourself and resist this dangerous impulse. The Bible says that God will create self-control in you Himself, so ask the Lord for help. He will remind you to walk away when you need to. And He will provide you with self-control and also with "love, joy, peace, patience, kindness, goodness, faithfulness, gentleness, and self-control" (Galatians 5:22-23) – everything you need to avoid the pitfalls of unfettered emotions.

A gentle answer turns away wrath,
but a harsh word stirs up anger.

Proverbs 15:1

Having the same interests isn't crucial.

Bob & Louise Garnett

Married: May 25, 1942

Grinnell, Iowa

*Bob and Louise Garnett first met when her father picked up
Bob hitchhiking! Louise is very much a "homebody," yet Bob
has a number of outside interests, including a weekly television show
where he interviews older Americans.* "I wouldn't say Louise supports
my 'hobbies,' but she does tolerate them," Bob says, laughing.

※

Each person is unique. Learn to celebrate this in your marriage! Our
differences begin at conception. Every human being is lovingly fashioned
by God to be special, distinct, unlike anyone else – and therefore precious
in His sight. Long ago, King David said, "You shaped me first inside, then
out; you formed me in my mother's womb. I thank you, High God – you're
breathtaking! Body and soul, I am marvelously made!" (Psalm 139:13-14 MSG).

86

Spouses sometimes share a few similarities. But God often joins two people who have vastly different strengths, weaknesses, talents, interests, personalities, and perspectives. The character traits of each spouse complement the other, making the couple stronger, expanding their potential, and creating a life that they never could have known apart.

Consider for a moment this page. It has two main components: paper and ink. Think about how different their properties are. One is solid, one liquid. One is light, the other dark. One has a uniform appearance, the other flows into multiple shapes. Alone, both have function and intrinsic value, but together they acquire power to communicate!

You and your spouse are unique individuals, created and cherished by God, brought together according to His wisdom for His great purposes. *Vive la différence!*

Tell your spouse today of one quality you appreciate in them that you don't possess.

He created them male and female.

Genesis 1:27 msg

＊

Heartwarmers

Go window shopping
then buy ice cream.

Go on a date to the zoo.

Cuddle up in front of a
waterfall or fountain.

＊

Cultivate the ability to see each other's point of view.

John & Elenore Buchanan

Married: November 29, 1942

Great Falls, Montana

Elenore was a true "war bride" – she only knew John for two months
before they were married. John, a retired speech professor,
is an avid bicyclist. Elenore stays active with volunteer work.

※

Do you know the secret of holograms, 3-D movies, and depth perception? The answer is, it takes two! A split laser beam, a couple of camera lenses, a pair of eyes. With just one, all you get is a flat, one-dimensional image. Add another, and the result seems to jump off the page or leap out of the silver screen.

You need your spouse's viewpoint to more accurately perceive the world you live in. Ask for their input. With the insight your partner can provide, you will better understand not only your mate but also your children, other family members, your friends, coworkers, and associates. Your better half can help you sort out situations you are facing at work, evaluate investment opportunities that come your way, and decide which purchase decisions make the most sense. Best of all, your spouse can help you to see God more clearly, to experience His grace, to "grasp how wide and long and high and deep is the love of Christ" (Ephesians 3:18). Talk about 3-D!

And if two vantagepoints give you three dimensions, imagine what a third, omniscient viewpoint would contribute. Prayerfully seek the Lord's wisdom as you try to understand your spouse, attempt to relate to others, and in everything you do. A godly perspective will add an entirely new dimension to yours.

The Lord gives wisdom, and from his mouth
come knowledge and understanding.

Proverbs 2:6

Spend as much time together as possible.

Weslie & Marie Stable Sr.

Married: August 8, 1941

Gage, Oklahoma

Weslie and Marie were introduced by Weslie's sister –
a regular at the beauty shop where Marie worked. "We've had
ups and downs like anyone else," says Marie, "but we always
worked and prayed them through together." Wes owned a
grade-A dairy for years and still maintains hay fields.

In Matthew 19:1-12 Jesus teaches about the permanence of marriage, and in Malachi 2:16 God says outright, "I hate divorce!" (NLT). He knows the hurt and the scars people have from it. When a man and woman marry, they are meant to stay together.

However, God's intention for marriage is not simple longevity; but a happy, mutually fulfilling, lifelong union. Unfortunately, some couples' marriages long outlive their love. For one reason or another, perhaps for economic convenience or for the sake of their children, they remain married physically – but they have divorced emotionally. They inhabit the same house yet live separate lives.

Hopefully, your marriage is not like this! But amid all the hustle and bustle of everyday life, stop for a second and ask yourself, *Are my spouse and I behaving like a married couple these days, or more like roommates?*

One way to prevent the inner death of your marriage is to make sure you and your partner are spending enough time together. A relationship is a living thing, and time is the oxygen it requires. But in this fast-paced age, you have to *make* time for each other. So synchronize your appointment books. It's simply a matter of priority – you will always have time for the things most important to you.

Since they are no longer two but one, let no one separate them, for God has joined them together.
Matthew 19:6 nlt

Use the common sense God gave you.

Raymond & Bernice Bates

Married: May 17, 1941

Gentry, Arkansas

Raymond met Bernice when she was a young teacher boarding with his grandmother. "Folks these days are in too big a rush," Bernice says. "That's one reason they have so much trouble." In 1947 Raymond bought and rebuilt the creekside house in which they still live.

⋇

What is common sense, really? If we think of it in terms of public knowledge or universal opinion, we'd better be careful. Although many platitudes are rooted in Scripture and therefore sound enough to build a marriage on, there are a lot of "truisms" out there that aren't rooted in Scripture and will cause a marriage to crumble and fall. 1 Corinthians 3:19 says, "The wisdom of this world is foolishness in God's sight." So perhaps we'd better rework our definition.

The good sense we all have in common is, first, the truth God has revealed to humankind in the Bible and through His Son, Jesus Christ. Second, this good sense is the wisdom that God freely offers, relating to specific situations, if only we ask Him for it. Third, the God-given ability to reason with our minds and make wise choices based on the truth and wisdom He has provided us is also part of our good sense.

The Lord has made this type of common sense available to us all – let's thank Him for it and honor Him by using it! One practical way to do this is to read one verse from the book of Proverbs every day, meditate upon it, and put it into practice in your marriage. You'll be amazed at how sensible God's words of wisdom turn out to be.

Who endowed the heart with wisdom
or gave understanding to the mind?
Job 38:36

Feel lucky to be married!

Lou & Marsha Vabner

Married: October 12, 1941

Las Vegas, Nevada

Lou and Marsha are strong believers in commitment and conflict resolution. Lou says if an argument occurs that makes you want to get separated or divorced, then you're not handling the situation correctly.

❖

Sitting at a red light in your unwashed minivan, listening to the kids fighting and the mind-numbing songs from the *Toddler Tunes* cassette, it's hard not to be envious of the person who pulls up in a shiny, bright-red convertible, top down, CD player pumping out real, adult music. *Probably single,* you think, fighting pangs of jealousy as the light turns, and you're left in the dust.

Or perhaps you don't have any children, but lately you feel as if you've been tied to the fence and forced to stand there nibbling nubs of grass while the rest of the herd gallops off across the wide open plain. *Ah, freedom,* you sigh, *greener pastures!*

Remind yourself that in most cases, the reason why so many others are running hard and fast is that they're lonesome and longing for something you already have. Think back – you remember that feeling! But "God places the lonely in families" (Psalm 68:6 NLT), and He has set you in a loving relationship with the special person He has chosen just for you. Your spouse is heaven-sent, a priceless gift from above. You are truly blessed!

You haven't been confined to the corral; you've been saddled up for one of life's greatest rides. The thrills are subtle – but the joys run deep. Dedicate yourself to this journey that is like no other.

Rejoice in the wife of your youth. . . .
May you always be captivated by her love.
Proverbs 5:18-19 nlt

Always try to please each other.

Leroy & Dorothy Walker

Married: January 17, 1941

Old Fort, North Carolina

Leroy and Dorothy are one of three couples created when three brothers married three sisters. "It might make for a confusing genealogy someday!" Leroy says, laughing. The couple enjoys camping, reading, and playing table games.

What delights your spouse? Are you aware of the things that put a smile on their face, a sparkle in the eyes? Do you know how to gladden your spouse's heart and bring pleasure, gratification, and contentment?

Try to discover what pleases your partner. It begins with getting to know your spouse better and better, through observation and communication as you spend time together. Pinpoint your mate's needs and desires. Then, as you go about your daily lives, do your best to satisfy both.

98

A good way to please your spouse is to meet their expectations. If it's your turn to do the dishes, make sure they get done! Even better, exceed expectations. After you've washed the dishes, dried them, and put them away, sweep and mop the floor, then clean the kitchen windows. Perhaps the best way is to do the unexpected. Do all this sometime when it's *not* your turn – then leave a bouquet of flowers on the table!

Remember the Golden Rule, and do for your mate what would please you: a service, a gift, a gesture of affection, anything that demonstrates to your partner that you were thinking of them and wanted to please. That's the real key. Your desire to make your spouse happy will brighten their day and leave them feeling loved.

Let each of us please his neighbor for his good,
leading to edification.

Romans 15:2 nkjv

Don't get mad over little things – they'll soon pass.

Gerald & Helen Brown

Married: July 20, 1941

Fairview, Illinois

Gerald and Helen first "got cozy" when he drew her name at a Valentine's party. "Actually, it was more of a box supper – and I'm still fixing him supper every night!" Helen jokes. In addition to sharing meals, the two enjoy playing card games together.

Newspaper advice columns often print letters complaining about a spouse's snoring or some other small irritation. But whenever those letters appear, they are soon followed up with letters from widows and widowers with statements like these: "I used to hate my husband's snoring, but now that he's gone, I would give anything to have him lying beside me during the night – snoring and all." Or they write, "My wife used to nag me about my appearance. But since she died, I can see that no one cares about me the way she did." These people have learned that in the end, those little marital irritations mean less than nothing.

You and your spouse are distinctly different individuals – that's the way God created you. One of you may be laid back and messy, while the other may be intense and obsessively neat. One of you may be fun loving and friendly, while the other is serious and empathetic. All these types are guaranteed to produce irritations. But that doesn't mean you have to focus on them.

Don't get angry about little things. Let God help you gain a deep appreciation for your spouse – even for those things that make you crazy.

Love covers over all wrongs.

Proverbs 10:12

Forget TV and spend time with each other.

Joe & Pauleen Karner

Married: July 8, 1940

Mesilla Park, New Mexico

*Joe and Pauleen started having "family worship" the night
they were married. A few years later Joe became a minister.
Pauleen loves the piano (she taught for twelve years);
Joe enjoys gardening and "inventing things" in his workshop.*

⁂

Imagine if Joe and Pauline, who found individual pursuits that are worthwhile and fulfilling, had come together at the end of each day and spent most evenings of their married life sitting in front of the TV, staring at the screen instead of connecting with each other in a meaningful way. What would be the quality of their relationship after more than sixty years?

Fortunately, they are wise enough to avoid the dangers of too much television and focus on each other, so they can enjoy not only their own personal hobbies but also the many benefits of a rich, healthy marriage. They know the importance of maintaining a good balance between time for themselves and time for each other – and they know that this means limiting time for the TV. Get the picture?

Go further. Discover in your times of "family worship" the joy of spending time together with God, as well. There is no activity that will draw a husband and wife closer than praying to the Lord and worshiping Him as a couple. When a man and a woman open their hearts to God, their hearts are opened to each other, and such tender intimacy fosters the deepest level of bonding.

Don't allow a TV set to rob you and your spouse from the blessings of a marriage blessed by God!

Oh, get up, dear friend, my fair and beautiful lover –
come to me!
Song of Songs 2:13 msg

Spend quality time together every day – even if it's just a few minutes.

Ron & Sally Metsbeth

Married: May 7, 1940

Gallup, New Mexico

Ron and Sally first met at a church social. "And we've been pretty sociable ever since!" Sally laughs. Both are avid Scrabble players.

※

He rushes through the kitchen toward the hall closet, where he grabs his coat. "Have you seen my keys?" he asks as he searches the coat pockets. She spots them on the counter and brings them to him, holding their two-year-old in one arm and cradling the cordless phone against her shoulder. "The doctor says to give her ibuprofen and keep checking her temperature," she says. "If the fever gets much worse, we may have to take her in." He picks up his briefcase. "Okay. I've got to run." She ends her call and gives a little wave as he heads for the door.

Halfway out he suddenly stops. He turns and sets down his briefcase, then hugs his wife and kisses her. After a moment she pulls away, but he holds her tight in a prolonged embrace. Finally the toddler begins to squirm, and he steps back, taking her from his wife. "Are you doing all right?" he asks, looking into his wife's eyes.

"Well, I'm concerned about our daughter," she answers.

He nods and says, "I'll tell you what. I'll keep in touch throughout the morning, and we'll decide together what to do. Okay?" She smiles and agrees.

Sometimes emotional connection takes just a moment, yet it means so much. Even on the busiest of days, be sure to grab that moment.

There is a time for everything,
and a season for every activity under heaven.
Ecclesiastes 3:1

Don't take things too seriously.

Curt & Jonnie Palat

Married: April 7, 1940
Greenville, South Carolina

Curt and Jonnie met at the grocery store. "I invited her to church," Curt says, "and we still go to church together today!" They often spend their mornings looking into each other's eyes over Danishes at McDonald's.

❋

Husbands, how are you going to handle it when your wife bangs up the side of the car while backing out of the garage? Wives, how will you react when your husband tries to fix the washing machine and ends up flooding the basement, ruining the brand-new carpet?

The quicker you can see humor in a stressful situation, the better for your marriage!

This is especially true with situations that involve destruction or loss of material possessions. Why lay blame and struggle with guilt and bitterness? Since nobody was hurt, the damage is already done, and you know you'll be telling jokes about the disaster someday, why not just have a good laugh over it now and move on?

Laughter takes faith. It requires trust in God, who has unlimited resources and has promised to provide for our needs. Somehow or other He will come through for us. A person who trusts God's promises and believes in His power to fulfill them "laughs with no fear of the future" (Proverbs 31:25 NLT).

Studies have shown that humor and laughter promote physical healing. They certainly are a balm for the soul. So the next time things are amiss, just shake your head and chuckle – and think of the stories you'll tell.

A cheerful heart is good medicine.

Proverbs 17:22 nlt

Always keep your communication open and honest.

Ralph & Earline Moore
Married: August 29, 1940

Madison, Tennessee

Ralph and Earline got acquainted during a Saturday night college social.
"He claims when I came into the room, he knew I was the girl
he was to marry," she says. Both share a lifelong love of traveling
and still manage to take at least four or five trips a year.

※

"I tell you the truth . . ." Jesus often began. Then He would do just that. Sometimes He would offer wonderful promises, and sometimes He would deliver hard truths. He didn't always tell the people what they wanted to hear, but He never failed to say what they needed to hear. Jesus modeled open and honest communication.

It's critical that you and your spouse keep the dialogue flowing in your marriage, and that you are straightforward with each other. You can resolve most problems with honest, heartfelt communication. You may need outside help in a time of crisis, but it all starts with honesty. On the other hand, dishonesty or not communicating can shipwreck any marriage.

There are times when you and your partner will have discussions that are painful and difficult. It will take a lot of courage. But don't shy away from speaking with compassion and sensitivity, as Jesus did, and working things through. Seek the help of a pastor, Christian counselor, or trusted friend if necessary.

In any case, invite God into your conversation. He will guide you through the chaos; and you and your spouse will emerge from the experience stronger, more united, and with a deeper understanding of and love for one another.

Kings take pleasure in honest lips;
they value a man who speaks the truth.
Proverbs 16:13

Never be the first one to get angry.

Knud & Ruth Hansen

Married: April 9, 1940
Copenhagen, Denmark

Knud and Ruth dated during World War II. Because she was from
Norway and living in Denmark, their love letters were censored
by the government. According to Ruth, "They were going to deport me,
so we had to get married!" She adds that they've been in love
all their lives and enjoy walking together and visiting friends.

Instead of being the "fastest gun in the West" with your anger, strive
to be the first to work at resolution and reconciliation. Proverbs 15:18 says,
"Those who are hot-tempered stir up strife, but those who are slow to
anger calm contention" (NRSV). The title of peacemaker is much nobler!

Try to determine if the problem is the result of poor communication or
a simple misunderstanding. Recently a mother got into a heated debate with

her three-year-old daughter while discussing an upcoming road trip. The daughter seemed to be insisting that she did not want to be buckled into her car seat. "Stand!" she kept saying. The mother told her firmly, "You will have to sit!" The daughter responded in frustration, "Stand!" The argument escalated until the mother suddenly realized that the little girl was trying to say, "I don't understand!"

Sometimes people struggle to find the right words to express a deeply felt need or emotion. They may not even quite understand what they are feeling inside. It may be up to you to ask thoughtful, probing questions and then listen intently for the real message behind your beloved's words.

If you are too quick on the draw with your temper, you'll miss this opportunity for constructive communication and deepening your love – and you had better take cover, because things are going to fly!

Blessed are the peacemakers,
for they will be called sons of God.

Matthew 5:9

When you marry, commit for a lifetime!

Herman & Bernice Walker

Married: June 9, 1940

Old Fort, North Carolina

Herman and Bernice met when she was fourteen and he was nineteen.
"Some of the other boys would get fresh," she remembers,
"but Herman was always a perfect gentleman." The couple
enjoys gardening and listening to country music.

Often grown children of divorced parents approach marriage with a deep appreciation for the value of lifelong commitment. They've endured firsthand the trauma of divorce, having felt the earth-shaking tremors and witnessed the collapse of their home, and they're determined not to go through it again – or put their own children through it. Most of us, if we haven't ourselves been at the epicenter of divorce, have sensed the after-shocks among our extended family, our circle of friends, or our associates.

Like the children of divorce, we would do well to learn from our experience and take the promises of matrimony to heart.

When you speak your wedding vows, make a deep commitment to God, your spouse, and yourself to keep them for life. Decide in the core of your being that you are in this relationship for better or for worse, come what may.

A powerful way to reinforce your commitment over time is to renew your vows on a regular basis. You can do this every year, in a solemn personal ceremony in the privacy of your own home. Or every few years, perhaps on significant anniversaries, you can reaffirm publicly your dedication to one another.

Marriage is a covenant and it is sacred to God. You will honor the Lord, and He will honor you, if you stay true to your promise.

Guard yourself; remain loyal to the wife of your youth.

Malachi 2:15 nlt

Learn how to talk things over.

Kermit & LaRue Burrough

Married: June 15, 1939

Berryville, Arkansas

Kermit and LaRue have spent their lives operating a dairy and strawberry farm established by his parents. "Country life is ideal," says LaRue, "especially if you can find a man like my Kermit – kind, honest, clean-living, and a hard worker."

When two people get married, they need to find a way to understand each other, or the relationship will soon be in trouble. If they are wise, they will do one of two things: either learn to read minds or polish their communication skills.

A common problem couples face is that both spouses think their partner ought to be able, in some mysterious way, to perceive what they are thinking and feeling. For whatever reason, at some point the idea *If he loves me, he should know what I need – without my having to tell him!* gets implanted in their heads. And of course, this expectation goes unspoken.

Words are mighty tools for nurturing intimacy, maintaining unity, resolving conflict, and sharing hopes and dreams. Language, the ability to express our deepest thoughts and sentiments and reveal our true inner selves through the spoken word, is a beautiful gift from our loving Creator. We mustn't neglect it!

Real communication goes beyond words. It includes eye contact, tone of voice, and body language. And there are two main components to the act of communication: talking and listening. The latter is not a passive activity; it is an active process that should be practiced and mastered. Learn to listen well, and you will be amazed at what you will discover in your spouse's heart and soul.

The words of a man's mouth are deep waters.

Proverbs 18:4 nkjv

Learn to love and appreciate the good in each other.

Joseph & Lenora Holland

Married: November 2, 1939

Watts, Oklahoma

Joseph was a carpenter when he married Lenora. He served in World War II as a combat engineer and later became a pastor.

Are people basically good or bad?

The Bible's answer to this philosophical question is "both." God's Word clearly states that every person inherited the nature of Adam and Eve, who committed the original sin by disobeying God in the Garden of Eden. However, all of us share something else with our famous ancestors: we bear the image of God. When the Lord created human beings, he declared them to be very good.

In relating to our spouse, the question is, should we focus on the good or the bad? The answer is, both. We must accept the whole person, imperfection and all.

However, you'll want to celebrate your spouse's positive qualities. Express your appreciation for their admirable traits, and congratulate your spouse on the things they do well. You will encourage your partner and foster their continued character development.

Deal with the negative aspects of your spouse in the same way God chooses to handle imperfection – gracefully and lovingly. Proverbs 10:12 says, "Love covers over all wrongs." Don't deny that your mate is imperfect or pretend that a problem doesn't exist. Talk about it openly and honestly, extend forgiveness, and look for ways to help your spouse grow in this area as well.

Embrace your beloved *as is*, warts and all, with every virtue and vice. However, cherish, accentuate, and build upon the positive.

Love does not delight in evil but rejoices with the truth.

1 Corinthians 13:6

Always respect one another.

B. J. & Anita Kohler

Married: August 27, 1939

Copenhagen, Denmark

*B. J. and Anita were married in Europe just one week
before the outbreak of World War II. Today they travel
frequently and enjoy visiting with friends.*

Parents of young children are often reminded – as when their five-year-old demands, "Get me something to eat!" – of the value of good manners. It's surprising how much difference a simple "please" can make. Simple gestures of politeness go a long way in helping people interact smoothly and harmoniously.

Married couples sometimes need to be reminded that it's important to continue showing each other the same consideration they did when they were dating. One of the reasons why courtship is so romantic is that starry-eyed lovers are always on their best behavior, treating each other with decency and respect. Their every word and action indicates that they value and appreciate one another.

Practicing politeness requires forethought and effort, however. It's interesting to note that good manners do not come naturally – children must learn and then practice them. Youngsters tend to think of themselves first, before considering others' needs. As adults, unfortunately, we are not entirely free of that inclination. Human nature sometimes causes us to indulge in selfish, disrespectful, immature behavior – which only leads to hurt feelings and resentment. Nobody likes to be treated rudely or taken for granted.

Daily offering your spouse simple tokens of respect conveys esteem, recognition, and regard. It validates the dignity and worth of the person you love the most.

Respect everyone and show special love for God's people.

1 Peter 2:17 cev

If you can't change something, learn to live with it.

Kermit & Phyllis Foss

Married: January 21, 1939

Minneapolis, Minnesota

*Kermit and Phyllis believe that opposites attract for a reason.
"He's always calming me down," says Phyllis, "or I would have
burned out years ago!" Kermit is an ordained minister, and
over the years they've served in fourteen different states.*

∗|∗
∙

There are people living in the northern states who, if they had their
druthers, would move to Florida, where the weather is pleasant year
round and they wouldn't have to deal with ice and snow and freezing
temperatures. Some of them withdraw into their homes during the cold
season and curse Old Man Winter. But others have learned that the best
way to beat the winter doldrums is to dress warmly, go outside, and

get involved in some of the exciting activities that only snowy weather can offer.

There are people living down south who think it's too hot and miss the beauty of the changing seasons. They remember the colors of autumn, the splendor of a bright winter morning, the thrill of watching the earth return to life each spring. Some of them bemoan their environment and long to be elsewhere. But others put on the sunscreen and head for the beach or the golf course and take full advantage of the warm climate.

There is no perfect place to live. And there will always be some aspect of your situation that you wish were different, whether it be something about your home, your neighborhood, your workplace, your city - or even your spouse. Many of these things are beyond your power to change. So learn to make the best of things!

I have learned in whatever state I am, to be content.
Philippians 4:11 nkjv

Learn from others. Good family role models can help.

Albert & Ophelia Rodarte

Married: November 29, 1939

Watts, California

Both Albert's and Ophelia's families provide good examples. Ophelia's sister was married to Albert's brother for fifty-three years. Her parents were also married for life, and her dad lived to age ninety-three.

God's Word comes to us in a multitude of ways. He has made His wisdom for living available in written form, the Bible, so we can learn to love each other and please Him. The Gospels tell about the life of Jesus, God's Word in human form, our ultimate role model for right living. However, God's Word becomes particularly meaningful, powerful, and effective in our lives today when it is manifested in the people around us. Members of our family who have chosen to follow Christ and have allowed God's Word to sink into their hearts and actions have a dramatic impact on our lives as we listen to them, observe their behavior, and strive to walk in their footsteps.

The apostle Paul wrote, "Follow my example, as I follow the example of Christ" (1 Corinthians 11:1). God wants us to benefit from the faithful role models He has placed in our lives. If the Lord has blessed you with family members who set a godly example in their work, their play, their relationships, and their marriage, learn from them and try hard to emulate them.

God created the family as a potent means of molding character and teaching about life. Good family role models can lead us on the right path and help us become people worth following.

He did what was right in the eyes of the LORD,
just as his father David had done.

2 Kings 18:3

Marry a hard worker and a good provider.

James & Rosa Belle Clemmons

Married: January 21, 1938

Etowah, North Carolina

James and Rosa Belle met through her father. "He worked in Daddy's cotton mill," she says. "Daddy hired him, and I married him!" Both have enjoyed many years of fishing and going on picnics.

Ladies, you've heard this time-honored counsel before, and it's worth heeding. A hard-working nature is the hallmark of a godly man, and the Lord will use such a man to provide for your needs for food, clothing, and shelter, making you feel loved and safe and secure. The alternative is not good. According to Ecclesiastes 10:18, if you marry a lazy man, your house will be in poor repair. You may end up carrying an umbrella indoors – if the roof doesn't cave in altogether!

But gentlemen, this is good advice for you as well. Proverbs 31 describes a wife of noble character, and she is depicted as a woman who applies herself to her duties with enthusiasm, intelligence, and vigor. Not one to be idle, she works hard to care for her family and diligently manages the affairs of her home. "Her husband can trust her, and she will greatly enrich his life" (Proverbs 31:11 NLT). Both he and their children consider her blessed.

Maintaining a healthy marriage relationship is, in and of itself, hard work. So is earning money, keeping up the house and yard, raising children, and a myriad of other chores that come with married life. Find a mate who is up to the task, and together you can work hard to build a home.

Those who work hard will prosper and be satisfied.
Proverbs 13:4 nlt

Learn to be content with what you have.

Culver & Virginia Wilber

Married: June 16, 1938
Urbandale, Michigan

Culver and Virginia got together because Culver decided that she
"was the one." "He picked me out first," Virginia adds, "and I fell
for him later!" Their evening routine includes watching the
news while they eat supper, then watching Jeopardy.

⁒

God's tenth commandment says, "Do not covet your neighbor's house . . . or anything else your neighbor owns" (Exodus 20:17 NLT). But what about family and friends?

Sometimes the desire to keep pace with them is more of a problem than wanting to keep up with the Joneses. The Lord may bless our friends and the members of our extended family differently from the way He blesses us. These are the people we are closest to, the people we relate to and identify with most. When we see them prosper financially and begin to enjoy more and better material possessions, we may struggle with conflicting emotions. Of course we are happy for them and rejoice with them in their good fortune, but despite ourselves we may also experience pangs of jealousy that lead to discontentment with the things God has given us.

The only cure for envy and discontentment is gratitude. If you are wrestling with these feelings, try adopting a "desert island" perspective. Envision yourself living with your immediate family, with all your belongings, on an otherwise uninhabited island. There's no one else in sight, nobody to compete with, nothing to compare your possessions to. Imagine how thankful you would be for each blessing the Lord has bestowed!

The key to contentment is to focus gratefully on what God has done for you.

A heart at peace gives life to the body,
but envy rots the bones.

Proverbs 14:30

Spend quality time with your spouse and children.

Kenneth & Dorothy Emerson

Married: June 19, 1938

Angwin, California

Kenneth and Dorothy sat next to each other alphabetically in school.

※

It's always a challenge to find time to spend with your partner, your kids, even with the Lord. But there is one surefire strategy you can employ to *make* the time you need in order to nurture your most important relationships: simplify your life.

One of the easiest, most effective ways to do this is to get rid of some possessions. The things we own require a great deal of our time, effort, and money. Much of the busyness in our lives is dictated by the need to pay for, insure, maintain, and repair our material assets. Our possessions also rob us of mental and emotional energy as we think and worry about where we'll keep them, how we'll take care of them, and how much over-time we'll have to put in to pay off the credit cards we used to buy them.

God wants us to adopt His priorities, which are to love Him and love each other. Jesus told a harried woman named Martha, whose sister Mary was sitting attentively at His feet, "You are worried and upset about many things, but only one thing is needed. Mary has chosen what is better" (Luke 10:41-42).

Making time for relationships involves making some choices. Choose wisely and simplify your life so you can spend time with God and your family.

Sell your possessions and give to the poor...
Then come, follow me.

Matthew 19:21

Heartwarmers

Attend a concert in the
park – or make your own!

Watch an old movie together.

Take a leisurely drive and
enjoy the scenery.

Learn to roll with the punches.

Lennie & Victoria Shane

Married: January 29, 1938

Tujunga, California

Lennie is a real-life cowboy who has worked horses and livestock all his life.

∙ゝゝ

When a cowboy is thrown from the saddle, he can either tense his muscles, stiffen his arms, and resist the fall – or he can relax his body and hit the ground rolling. If he tenses up, he runs the risk of further injury, perhaps torn ligaments or broken bones. But if he rolls with the impact, often he will be able to spring right back up, remount his horse, and ride on.

A man named Saul, a devout Jew, once took a fall *because* he was resisting. He was fighting Christianity with all his might, hunting down Christians so they could be imprisoned, tried, and put to death. On his way to Damascus, he saw a great light, fell to the ground, and heard the resurrected Jesus say, "Saul, Saul, why do you persecute me? It is hard for you to kick against the goads" (Acts 26:14). Eventually Saul stopped opposing the church, accepted God's will for his life, and proclaimed the gospel far and wide as the apostle Paul – an unbelievable change of heart.

When you and your spouse face adversity, pray for the wisdom to know whether to stand firm or roll with the punches. Perhaps God is working powerfully in your circumstances to bring about His plans for you and take you places you cannot now begin to imagine.

God causes everything to work together
for the good of those who love God.

Romans 8:28 nlt

Focus on the things that matter, and let the little things slide.

Tex & Donnetta Taylor

Married: December 12, 1938

Dallas, Texas

Tex and Donnetta were born in the same town just a few days apart.
They still remember playing together as children in her backyard.

⁂

Life gets awfully busy. This is true whether we're helping our spouse finish college, parenting young children, or moonlighting to make ends meet. At times it's easy to become frustrated and depressed because the house is always dusty, the furniture is looking worn, the curtains in the bedroom don't match the colors in the bedspread, and the car door is starting to rust.

It's hard not to focus on problems like these and begin to devote our time, energy, and resources to fixing them. Yet if we don't learn to let them go and keep our attention on the things that really matter, we may neglect the emotional needs of our spouse and our children.

God wants us to trust Him for everything, and from His perspective even life's essentials are little things. Jesus said, "Do not worry, saying, 'What shall we eat?' or 'What shall we drink?' or 'What shall we wear?' . . . Seek first [God's] kingdom and his righteousness, and all these things will be given to you" (Matthew 6:31, 33).

At the end of the day, be thankful that the Lord has provided you and your family with a roof over your head, clothes to wear, and food to eat. And be grateful that He has freed you from the need to worry, so you can focus on what's truly important.

Having food and clothing, with these we shall be content.
1 Timothy 6:8 nkjv

Keep two cozy chairs side by side, and enjoy time each day just sitting together.

Edward & Thelma Cogswell

Married: March 4, 1937

Washington, D.C.

Thelma met Edward at his parents' dry goods store. She stopped to buy a fancy handkerchief to match her party dress, but the store had just closed. Edward let her in anyway.

※

He closes the sliding glass door with one hand, holding two cups of coffee with the other. Carefully he makes his way to where she is sitting on their back deck, watching the orange of the sunset begin to fade. Their favorite sitting place is nothing fancy, just a couple of comfortable patio chairs on the old wooden deck they jokingly refer to as "the west terrace."

It's where they like to spend a few moments together every evening, just being together and enjoying the beauty of God's creation.

The phone rings inside the house, but they let the answering machine pick it up. "Kids are asleep," he says with a grin, handing her a cup. "Thanks," she says, smiling. As he sits beside her, she thinks about how glad she is that they made a pact a long time ago to leave the TV off for an hour after the children were put to bed, to give themselves some time to sit outside, unwind from the day, and connect.

They chitchat and laugh, enjoying the cool air and each other's company as they watch the stars come out. For a while each evening they shut out all distractions and focus on one another. They belong to each other and no one else. She sips her coffee and reflects, *It's a gift we've given ourselves.*

My lover is mine, and I am his.
Song of Songs 2:16 msg

To have a good marriage, work as a team.

Ervin & Kathleen Langley

Married: June 21, 1937

Springdale, Arkansas

Ervin and Kathleen met in a blackberry patch between their Ozark Mountain homes. Even though Ervin worked and Kathleen stayed at home with their five children, they still tackled everything as a team.

※

A precise division of labor can be very helpful to your marriage relationship. Deciding together who will take care of which chores around the home ensures that you and your spouse agree on which tasks need to be done and who will be responsible for them. This lays a framework of clear expectations and accountability to one another.

138

Without such an agreement, things can slip through the cracks and go undone, and you may end up pointing fingers at each other, arguing over who is to blame.

When assigning tasks, take into account each partner's strengths and weaknesses. This is a more important consideration than traditional gender roles. If one of you is better with numbers than the other, for example, that person should be the one to maintain the checkbook and keep track of your finances. Decisions regarding income, spending, investing, and borrowing will of course be made together, so communicating with one another about the state of your finances is important. But paying the bills, balancing the checkbook, and other such duties can, and probably should, be handled by one person alone.

Teamwork is the name of the game. Both of you will benefit when you work together to maintain a happy home, each of you faithfully pulling your share of the load, counting on each other to get the job done.

Everyone who planted the seed and everyone
who harvests the crop will celebrate together.
John 4:36 cev

Pray with each other and for each other daily.

Michael & Jean Duras

Married: July 15, 1937

Krakow, Poland

Michael and Jean met when she was visiting her mother's family in Poland. "Michael was a factory engineer," says Jean. "He heard there was an American in the area and wanted to learn English." After they were married, they lived in Poland for twelve years, then moved to Detroit.

※

Praying with your spouse has an immediate, strong emotional effect on you. Not only are you privy to your partner's inner self as they pours out needs and desires to God, but when your mate begins to pray for you, asking the Lord to grant your deepest longings and help you in your most guarded areas of weakness, you are struck by how well you are known, how thoroughly you are understood, and how much you are loved.

However, prayer is so much more than an emotional experience. As you pray for your loved ones, you are inviting almighty God to act in their lives, to move in their circumstances, to mold their characters, to change the very attitudes of their heart. You are unleashing the power of God to protect and provide, to nurture and guide and bless. What more meaningful thing could you do for the people you cherish?

Proverbs 15:8 says, "[The LORD] delights in the prayers of the upright" (NLT). This scripture provides a powerful incentive for godliness. When we realize that our conduct affects the way God hears our prayers for ourselves, our spouse, and our children, we begin to recognize the eternal ramifications of our sinfulness. Thankfully, though, Jesus offers His righteousness in exchange for our imperfection – and when we make the trade, our prayers become music to God's ears.

The earnest prayer of a righteous person
has great power and wonderful results.

James 5:16 nlt

Busy hands make for a good marriage.

Darrell & Ethel Elder
Married: October 18, 1937
Fayetteville, Arkansas

Darrell and Ethel have been farming all their lives.
"I could do everything except shoe a horse!" exclaims Ethel.
In addition to keeping up with a dairy and huge garden,
Darrell started one of the area's first commercial chicken operations.

It's good to be busy, but not *too* busy. As with so many things in life, it's all a matter of degree. The Bible commends diligence but warns against working too much; it offers rest for the weary and sleep for God's loved ones yet condemns excessive idleness. So where do you draw the line?

The answer is to ask the Lord to give you and your spouse the wisdom to maintain a healthy, balanced lifestyle. Work hard but learn to relax too. Enjoy good food but do so in moderation. Exercise regularly but don't overdo it. Get the sleep you need but don't become a sluggard.

Balance your time together with time to yourselves, time with your children, time with friends, and time with the Lord. Balance spending to meet your needs with giving to supply the needs of the poor. Balance looking after your interests with considering the well being of others. Balance seriousness with laughter, the newspaper headlines with the funny pages, news reports with comedy and cartoons, praying about the world's problems with enjoying the wonders of God's creation.

If the scale of busyness must tip one way or the other, however, it's a safe bet to lean toward working hard. If idleness truly is the Devil's playground, then it's better to keep yourself occupied with worthwhile pursuits and stay out of trouble.

Sow your seed in the morning,
and at evening let not your hands be idle.

Ecclesiastes 11:6

Don't try to change each other.

Don & Gladyce Kroll

Married: July 2, 1937

Soldier, Iowa

Don and Gladyce first met at a high school basketball game.
They still share a love of sports and often
watch ball games together on television.

※

There are core aspects of each individual that are hardwired into their personality. No matter how hard you try, you won't ever be able to change them. You will never turn someone who is basically reserved into a person who is naturally outspoken and gregarious. A generally detail-oriented person will always struggle when dealing with abstract, nebulous circumstances.

Every personality trait has positive, beneficial qualities, as well as the potential to produce negative results. The downside of a good personality trait usually becomes apparent when it is carried to extremes. For example, a person imbued with strong leadership qualities and a decisive nature may go too far and step on others' toes. Someone with a great work ethic might go overboard and become a workaholic, bringing harm to the relationship with their spouse and children.

However, in His wisdom God brings into a marriage two people whose personalities mesh, supplementing each other's strengths, making up for each other's weaknesses, and moderating one another's tendency toward excess.

The secret is not to try to change the person the Lord gave you as your spouse but to receive them with acceptance, join with them enthusiastically, and help bring out the best of their God-given personality.

Honor God by accepting each other,
as Christ has accepted you.
Romans 15:7 cev

Never go to sleep angry.

Ralph & Dorothy Gustin

Married: November 6, 1937

Spokane, Washington

*When Ralph and Dorothy met, she was a student, and he was
her principal. They were married after Dorothy graduated.*

⋆

What goes through your head as you lie in bed at night? Are you
silently thanking the Lord for all He has done for you during the day? Or
are you quietly stewing over a disagreement you had with your spouse
that afternoon? Are you praying for your loved ones, asking God to bless
them and watch over them through the night, or are you mentally ticking
off a list of grievances your spouse has caused you and delineating each of
your partner's negative qualities?

Your mate may be fast asleep beside you, totally unaware of your
anger. Perhaps you failed to express it properly at the appropriate time,
and now it's all bottled up inside you. Or maybe you made your feelings

known but weren't able to completely forgive your spouse, and now you feel justified in holding on to at least some resentment. In any case, although your attitude will harm both of you in the long run, right now you are the one who is suffering and losing sleep.

Release your anger by fully and unconditionally forgiving your partner, tearing up your internal list of complaints, and meditating on your spouse's positive traits instead. God promises us forgiveness when we are willing to forgive others, and peace when we focus on the good in those around us.

Fix your thoughts on what is true and honorable and right. Think about things that are pure and lovely and admirable. Think about things that are excellent and worthy of praise.

Philippians 4:8 nlt

Make sure your dispositions fit. Don't just "fall in love."

Walter & Theone Wheeler

Married: September 3, 1937

St. Helena, California

Walter and Theone might never have gotten together if not for her piano teacher. "I had planned a career as a pianist," Theone says, "but she pointed out that he might make me happier than my piano. And he has!"

Romantic love is a glorious thing, but it will not serve as the foundation for a marriage. For starters, it has to do with emotions, and emotions are unreliable. As desirable as romantic feelings are, they are not a sound enough foundation on which to build a lifelong relationship. A marriage that will endure the test of time must rest on solid bedrock.

Genesis 24 tells the story of how Abraham, who was living among the ungodly inhabitants of a foreign land, sent a servant to his country to find a wife for his son Isaac from among his own people. Abraham wanted Isaac to marry a woman who would share his son's beliefs and be committed to his principles. God guided the servant to Rebekah, whose family was related to Abraham and knew the Lord. When the servant brought the girl to Isaac, "she became his wife, and he loved her" (Genesis 24:67). This couple experienced romance, but their relationship was based on something deeper.

Jesus stated that only the house built on His truth would stand. If you are thinking about getting married, consider the wisdom of His words. If your marriage is based on mutual faith in Christ, you and your spouse can rejoice that your home rests secure. And if it isn't, it's not too late to redo the foundation.

Be ye not unequally yoked together.

2 Corinthians 6:14 kjv

Be each other's very best friend.

Duncan & Gloria Eva

Married: July 4, 1937

Durban, South Africa

Duncan and Gloria have lived all over the world, from Zimbabwe to England. They continue to share a lifelong love of reading aloud to each other.

Perhaps the most compelling example of friendship in the Bible is that of David and Jonathan. They loved each other dearly; they took an oath of everlasting friendship; and Jonathan even gave David gifts as tokens of their bond. Their relationship is summed up in the words of 1 Samuel 18:1: "Jonathan became one in spirit with David, and he loved him as himself."

You and your spouse can and should be the best of friends. Like David and Jonathan, you can and should be soul mates. Follow their example and acknowledge your friendship. The next chance you get, take your partner by the hand and say, "You know, you really are my closest friend in the whole world." Express how much your friendship means to you. And once in a while, on no particular occasion, surprise your spouse with a gift to celebrate and commemorate your friendship.

Nurture the friendship component of your marriage by doing the things friends do: talking, having fun together, treating each other well, helping one another, standing up for each other, encouraging one another, forgiving each other.

Take time to reflect that, just as David and Jonathan cemented their friendship with a solemn vow, you and your spouse have permanently sealed your friendship within the sacred covenant of matrimony. You have become best friends for life.

The two of us have vowed friendship in GOD's name.
1 Samuel 20:42 msg

Determine from the start that divorce is never an option.

James & Mildred Garey

Married: December 26, 1936

Fulton, Kentucky

James and Mildred met at a high school play. "We both enjoyed dating in groups," says Mildred. The couple loves to camp and are currently driving the wheels off their fifth motor home!

Can a marriage even survive infidelity?

It can if both spouses are determined to save it, if both have committed themselves to the notion that no matter what happens, they will stay married and work it out. It's not easy – it will require openness, humility, repentance, forgiveness, hard work, time, and tears – but it's not impossible. And if the marriage does survive, though it will never be the same, it can emerge stronger from the ordeal.

Unfaithfulness is more often the result of an emotional disconnection between the spouses than mere physical attraction toward someone outside the marriage. For a variety of reasons – mostly stemming from a breakdown in communication – one or both partners begin feeling unvalued, unappreciated, unloved, and they begin to look elsewhere to meet their emotional needs. If the spouses can learn practical ways to express love for one another and meet each other's needs, the emotional connection can be reestablished, and the marriage relationship can be restored.

Although the Bible provides an "out" for a person whose spouse has been unfaithful, God's heart is that the marriage covenant be upheld and the couple be reconciled to one another. Each of us, in one way or another, has been unfaithful to God, yet He hasn't given up on us. He wants our marriages to reflect His nature like a mirror.

Go, show your love to your wife again,
though she is loved by another and is an adulteress.
Hosea 3:1

Remember, it's not important to always be right.

Gray & Madge Burleson

Married: July 11, 1936

Burnsville, North Carolina

Gray and Madge met at a church revival meeting,
where he was directing the choir. "He is the kindest,
gentlest person I've ever known," Madge says of her husband.

❊

The need to win every argument is a good indicator of a prideful nature. In contrast, a willingness to admit error points to a humble spirit. It's no secret as to which the Bible advocates. Proverbs 11:2 says, "Pride leads to disgrace, but with humility comes wisdom" (NLT).

Pride exacerbates dissent just as surely as do harsh, angry words, while humility promotes peaceful resolution. So the trick to reducing the amount and intensity of conflict in a marriage is, quite simply, to replace pride with humility.

We must examine the condition of our heart. If we discover that our attitude is one of stubbornness and pride, we should ask ourselves why. What is the root of our conceit? If we are honest with ourselves, we will often find that our pridefulness is a defense mechanism, a mask for feelings of uncertainty and inferiority. It's a substitute for having the courage to say, "I don't know" and risk losing the esteem of others. Pride is a stick we lean on to prop ourselves up; that's why it often goes before a fall.

Don't be afraid to admit that you don't have all the answers, and don't hesitate to confess when you're wrong. You don't need a flimsy crutch like pride to stand tall – God promises to lift up those who humble themselves.

Pride leads to arguments; those who take advice are wise.
Proverbs 13:10 nlt

Enjoy the simple things – like looking at sunsets.

Auburn & Louise Roland

Married: December 14, 1935

Leicester, North Carolina

Auburn and Louise did their courting on "walking dates."
"We lived out in the country," says Louise, "and neither family had a car."
Today they enjoy just driving around together, often stopping to eat out.

When you and your spouse feel the need to get back to basics, to look beyond the clutter and clamor of this bewildering, complicated world and see what really matters, just go outside together for a moment and gaze upward. No matter what time of day it is, you will witness God's splendor – and you'll be reminded that your primary purpose in living, the fundamental reason why the Lord created you both and brought you together, is to worship Him.

Psalm 19:1-2 says, "The heavens declare the glory of God; the skies proclaim the work of his hands. Day after day they pour forth speech; night after night they display knowledge." Whether you behold a sunrise or a sunset, whether the skies are blue or gray, whether you see a full moon or nothing but stars, whether the clouds are bunny rabbits or thunderheads – God made it all, and He is worthy of adoration.

Spend time with your spouse outdoors now and then, just enjoying the simple things, wondering at the beauty of God's awesome works, and doing what the Lord created you to do. And when a butterfly floats out of the sky and alights nearby, examine it closely and consider, *Who but God could have made such a lovely, "simple" thing?*

From the rising of the sun to the place where it sets,
the name of the LORD is to be praised.

Psalm 113:3

Be able to compromise when there is a difference of opinion.

Irving & Betty Filler

Married: September 15, 1935

Baltimore, Maryland

Irving and Betty first met while he was playing piano at a mutual friend's home. "Betty's a very kind person," says Irving. "I've never heard her say a bad word about anybody."

⁂

Here's a common dilemma between spouses: where to spend the holidays, with his family or hers? This is especially troublesome when both families are out of state, and visiting them involves a good deal of travel and expense. What if a couple with young children can only afford to make one trip per year? Whose parents will bounce grandchildren on their knees Christmas morning, and whose will have to settle for three-by-fives in their greeting cards?

Surely a compromise is in order. Working out an agreement that will satisfy both spouses requires communication, negotiation, creativity, and some give and take. After carefully listening to each other's needs and desires, both partners must be willing to make sacrifices to accommodate one another. Then a happy medium can be reached.

Perhaps the couple could visit his parents one year, hers the next. Maybe one year they could travel to his hometown for Easter and have her folks visit them for Christmas. Or they could find a midpoint some-where, everybody could travel a short distance and stay at a ski lodge, and they could all have a grand extended-family Christmas vacation!

Politics is the art of compromise – and so is marriage. Your willingness to compromise is an expression of your love for your spouse. It proves that you are concerned for your mate's happiness as well as your own.

Can two walk together, unless they are agreed?

Amos 3:3 nkjv

Do things together today – you may not have tomorrow.

Grant & Ruth Burch Jr.

Married: August 3, 1935

Anderson, Indiana

Ruth stood by Grant through a series of heart attacks, a brain tumor, partial kidney failure, and the loss of five fingers in a farming accident. Despite these challenges, he was active in local and state politics for over fifty years, raised Hereford cattle on a six-hundred-acre farm, and lovingly supported Ruth and their two children.

※

It's sad to think that you and your spouse must say goodbye someday. Not knowing when that will be gives you a powerful incentive to live each day as if it were the last you will share. It motivates you to appreciate each other, cherish one another deeply, and treat each other lovingly.

God wants you to live your lives to the fullest every day, enjoying each other and entrusting tomorrow to Him. However, this is not to say that you should live only for today, disregarding the future and adopting the philosophy, "Let us eat and drink, for tomorrow we die" (1 Corinthians 15:32). God wants you to live each day with the knowledge that you are eternal beings, and your choices have eternal consequences.

It is sad to contemplate the darkness of death, but if you choose to put your faith in Jesus Christ, you have a bright hope! You and your spouse may not have tomorrow here on earth, but you will enjoy an eternity in heaven with the God who loves you and created you. There will be endless happiness and joy, and wonder upon wonder for you to experience together.

The joy that you share today needn't be dimmed by the prospect of death; instead, it can shine with the promise of eternal life. It's your choice.

This is the day the LORD has made;
let us rejoice and be glad in it.

Psalm 118:24

Make your marriage a lifetime commitment.

Clyde & Lois Mae Franz

Married: June 2, 1935

Collegedale, Tennessee

Clyde and Lois Mae met at college when she broke up with a jealous boyfriend. "When I heard about it, I sent her a note asking her to meet me," Clyde says. "And she did!" The two enjoy camping, bird watching, and "anything else that gets us out into nature."

Now that you have spoken your wedding vows, now that you have made such high and lofty promises to each other before God and many witnesses, how do you intend to go about keeping those promises? You've made a lifetime commitment!

You can rely on your own resolve. You can trust your love for one another to see you through. You can seek the wisdom of others. You can follow the example of those who have gone before you. There are books to read, tapes to listen to, videos to watch, seminars to attend. Radio, TV, and the Internet can all be a source of information and advice.

But your most valuable resource is God. He is eternal, all-wise, all-powerful, never changing, always present, ever loving, holy, and good. He has the highest expectations for your marriage, yet He is always willing to help you meet them. God wants you to succeed! He is your greatest advocate. He wants your marriage to last a lifetime, for your benefit and because marriage glorifies Him.

And God doesn't desire to merely sit in the bleachers and cheer you along, shouting counsel and encouragement from afar. He wants to be on the gridiron, leading your team, calling the plays, sending you into the end zone for the winning pass, carrying you on His shoulders as you celebrate victory.

Help us, O LORD our God, for we rely on you.
2 Chronicles 14:11

Keep your priorities straight – responsibility ahead of pleasure.

Ed & Ruby Hallsted

Married: November 23, 1935

Fort Smith, Arkansas

Ed says when he was dating Ruby, he "tested" her by going to her house just after dinner one evening. When he asked if she wanted to go for a ride, Ruby said, "After I finish the dishes." "I guess I passed," Ruby says with a chuckle.

∿⁄╾

Marital bliss isn't all fun and games – never has been and never will be. Even Adam and Eve, living in the Garden of Eden, had work to do. And heaven will involve responsibilities as well as recreation.

Rule one is, work before play. Get your chores done, then have a good time. This is important to remember if you are the less responsible, more fun-loving partner. Playing while work goes undone will add to your spouse's stress, not alleviate it. (But remember, you overly responsible types: the work is never done. Learn when to quit and relax.)

Rule two is, needs before wants. Before you buy nonessentials, budget your money so you can pay bills, cover unexpected expenses, reduce debt, and save. When your finances are in order, you and your spouse can truly enjoy those little extras.

Rule three is, career before dream house. A home is a good investment, but don't jump in over your head. Establish your livelihood first, let that determine your standard of living, and be content with how the Lord has chosen to bless you.

Marriage involves a great deal of responsibility, but if you keep your priorities straight, it can be heavenly!

Develop your business first before building your house.
Proverbs 24:27 nlt

Marry someone who's a good cook!

Jeffrey & Lettieteen Blount Sr.

Married: March 17, 1934

Opelousas, Louisiana

Jeffrey worked in a huge oil refinery until his retirement.
For over thirty years Lettieteen carried lunch to him each day,
making his noon meal a special occasion.

※

They say that the way to a man's heart is through his stomach. That may or may not be true in love and marriage, but good food – delicious, satisfying, life-giving, and nutritious – *is* the key when it comes to a relationship with God, and such a relationship is the foundation of a good marriage. So even if you and your spouse are unfamiliar with recipe books, don't neglect to spend time and get acquainted with the Bible.

God's words themselves are food for the soul. Psalm 119:103 says, "How sweet are Your words to my taste, sweeter than honey to my mouth!" (NKJV). Not only will the Bible lead you and your mate to a closer relationship with your heavenly Father, but it contains a wealth of wisdom for nurturing and enhancing your relationship with each other. God designed marriage; let Him show you how to make it work!

The Bible will also point you to God's Son. Jesus said, "I am the bread of life. He who comes to Me shall never hunger. . . . If anyone eats of this bread, he will live forever" (John 6:35, 51 NKJV). In the Gospels we are introduced to Christ, we walk with Him and get to know Him, we hear His words and learn from Him. And in Him our deepest hunger is satisfied.

> *Eat what is good, and your soul*
> *will delight in the richest of fare.*
>
> **Isaiah 55:2**

꙳

Heartwarmers

Curl up on the couch and
look at wedding pictures.

Hold hands and watch
the sun set.

Share an ice cream
soda together.

꙳

Go with someone long enough before you marry to know who and what they are.

Wayne & Anne Barton

Married: April 7, 1934

Peoria, Illinois

Wayne and Anne first crossed paths working in the same business district. Anne says they dated a long time because of the Depression. "We finally decided it was never going to end," she jokes, "so we got married anyway!"

Words and behavior reveal a person's character. The only way to really get to know someone is to spend a long period of time with them, listening and observing to see how they deal with various situations.

For this reason, it's a good idea during courtship to do things together besides going out on dates. Spend time with the family of the person you're interested in, watching how they behave in a home environment. Volunteer your time at a nonprofit organization, work on a project, or baby-sit together. Listen, observe, and remember, "Out of the overflow of the heart the mouth speaks. The good man brings good things out of the good stored up in him" (Matthew 12:34-35).

Jesus said that one can always recognize a tree by its fruit, and a good tree will always produce good fruit. It takes time for fruit to develop, but inevitably it will, and only then can the tree be properly evaluated. Be patient!

For a Christian, to whom it is important to know that a potential spouse is also a believer, the surest indicator that another person truly knows and loves the Lord is the outward evidence of the presence of God's Spirit within. God's character will be displayed in the words and actions of His people.

The fruit of the Spirit is love, joy, peace, patience, kindness, goodness, faithfulness, gentleness and self-control.
Galatians 5:22-23

Learn to put up with his little quirks – he's learned to put up with yours.

Lloyd & Doris Mitchell

Married: September 1, 1934

Jay, Oklahoma

Doris first saw Lloyd as he drove his parents' covered wagon past her school on the way to a new homestead. "I told the other girls, 'That tall boy's mine!'" she remembers with a laugh. "And sure enough, he was!"

※

Whether traveling across the plains in a Conestoga wagon or touring the country in a motor home, spouses have always irritated each other. A woman whose husband insists on re-double-checking the tire pressure gets just as annoyed as the woman whose mate kept stopping to examine horseshoes.

If toothpaste came in tubes back then, surely one of the spouses squeezed it wrong. And it's a safe bet that at least one pair of socks got left on the prairie because some wife had had enough of her husband's habit of throwing his dirty clothes everywhere.

If it's a simple matter for you to change a little quirk that gets on your spouse's nerves, make the change. Anything you can do to promote harmony in your home will pay great dividends. Your partner will thank you, and you won't have to endure any more nagging.

And if your loved one regularly does some small thing that rubs you the wrong way, communicate your feelings constructively – once. Beyond that, overlook the behavior. Decide that it's not worth getting upset about and fighting over. Correct the "error" when and if necessary, joke about it occasionally, and choose to love your spouse all the more for their endearing foibles.

Rather than constantly pointing out your partner's faults, focus on what *you* can do to travel through life together peacefully.

Patiently put up with each other and love each other.
Ephesians 4:2 cev

Put each other first.
Do everything with your spouse in mind.

Clive & Dorothy Possinger

Married: November 29, 1934

Chester, Pennsylvania

Clive and Dorothy first became acquainted while he boarded at her parents'
house. They've shared a love of games all their lives and
say they've never been too busy for a good game of checkers.

⁂

There are two ways to go about marriage. One is to think about your needs; the other is to concentrate on the needs of your spouse. If each partner selfishly demands that the other meet their needs, the relationship will be characterized by disappointment, resentment, and bitterness. On the other hand, if each partner lovingly strives to fulfill the other's needs, the marriage will be characterized by mutual satisfaction, gratefulness, and joy.

That's God's way of doing things. The Bible says our attitude should be just like that of Christ, who, "being in very nature God," took on "the very nature of a servant" (Philippians 2:6-7). If anybody had a right to demand service, it was Jesus! But He loved his disciples enough to stoop and wash their feet.

You may fear that if you don't focus on your own needs, you'll be taken advantage of. But if you trust God's wisdom and focus on your partner's needs, the likelihood is that you'll be doubly blessed! When your spouse senses that you have their well-being in mind and are trying hard to meet their needs, your spouse will usually reciprocate enthusiastically. Plus, you'll find there is additional satisfaction and joy to be found in serving the one you love, because truly "it is more blessed to give than to receive" (Acts 20:35).

The Son of Man did not come to be served, but to serve.

Mark 10:45

Work hard but take time to play, too!

Herbert & Maxine Hatfield

Married: March 11, 1933

Bentonville, Arkansas

Herbert and Maxine started with a small gas station. Over the years, their business interests grew to include a car dealership, an insurance company, a car-leasing business, and several large real estate holdings. "We kept busy," laughs Maxine, "but we always took time to play along the way."

Have you ever seen those desktop pool tables, with their little cue sticks and tiny balls? It seems silly for a respectable businessperson to have one in the office, let alone play with it – yet it's amazing how relaxing, refreshing, and rejuvenating a few moments of fun in the middle of a hectic, stressful day can be. That must also explain dartboards, Nerf basketballs, and those hanging steel balls that knock each other back and forth.

We might think of taking time to play in terms of a full-blown vacation that includes travel, great dining, and lots of entertainment. But for many married couples, more often it means a weekend getaway, or just an hour or two in the evening, or maybe even simply a couple of stolen minutes of fun.

Don't burn yourself out with all work and no play, settling for daydreams about your big summer trip. Every now and then shut off the vacuum cleaner, sit down at the piano, and play a song. Close the word processor on your PC and double-click on a favorite computer game instead. Go for a short bike ride and enjoy the sunshine. Practice your putting.

Better yet, call your mate at work and say, "Honey, is there any way you can get out of your meeting this afternoon?" Your spouse is probably just shooting pool anyway.

God made everything beautiful in itself and in its time.

Ecclesiastes 3:11 msg

First make a commitment to the Lord, then to each other.

Melvin & Maggie Smith

Married: January 8, 1933

Chandler, Oklahoma

When they were teenagers, Melvin and Maggie worked in neighboring cotton fields. "The rows stopped at the fence," Maggie remembers with a grin, "so with a little timing, we could meet at the end of each row!" Melvin was a railway mail clerk for over thirty years; Maggie is a historian and author of twenty-four books.

Have you considered that when you stood before God, your loved one, and your community and took the vows of sacred matrimony, you not only made a promise to the Lord, your spouse, and the community, you stepped into an institution established by God? Marriage is His idea, His creation. He owns it, you've entered it, and you're bound to abide by His rules which govern it.

178

Marriage involves, first and foremost, a commitment to the Lord. He has taken another person, someone He cherishes, someone He created and nurtured and watched over and guided through the years, someone in whom He has invested a great deal and for whom He has wonderful plans; and He has entrusted that person to your care. His rules for marriage are meant to provide His dear one with a secure, loving environment in which to flourish.

God's rules for marriage are meant for your benefit, too, because He feels the same way about you. Marriage is a miracle in which the Lord joins two souls so they can experience a special kind of blessing, an inner growth, and an opportunity to glorify Him that they never would have known apart. Make a commitment to God and to your spouse that you will abide by His rules for marriage – and experience everything this miracle has to offer.

I have taken an oath and confirmed it,
that I will follow your righteous laws.
Psalm 119:106

Remember your vows. They're supposed to be true.

Ulyless & Zelma Ryburn

Married: October 21, 1933

Marktree, Arkansas

Zelma first saw Ulyless as he was rowing across a lake. "It was love at first sight for me," says Zelma, "but he dated others before he got around to asking me!" "I guess she just grew on me," says Ulyless with a wink. "Besides, I had more fun arguing with her than anyone else!"

᠅

If your child were to ask you what the stones on your wedding ring mean, would you be able to say precisely? Perhaps you could talk about how your ring symbolizes unending love, devotion, and commitment, but would you be able to remember and discuss all the promises you made to your spouse on your wedding day? If not, how do you know you are keeping all your vows?

After the Israelites crossed the Jordan River and entered the Promised Land, the Lord instructed them to pick twelve stones from the middle of the river, which he had caused to stop flowing, and set them up as a reminder of this miraculous event. God said, "In the future, when your children ask you, 'What do these stones mean?' tell them . . . " (Joshua 4:6-7). He meant for the stones to be a permanent memorial to His people of the specific events of that day.

Here's a thought: why not memorize your wedding vows? It wouldn't be any harder than learning the pledge of allegiance. You probably have them recorded somewhere, on paper or on video. Commit them to memory so that every time you look at your wedding ring, you can recite them, meditate on each one, and rededicate yourself to keeping them.

Remembering promises is so important that God himself makes it a priority.

Whenever the rainbow appears in the clouds, I will see it and remember the everlasting covenant between God and all living creatures of every kind on the earth.

Genesis 9:16

Don't be afraid to express your affection.

Gene & Francis Wood

Married: April 22, 1933

Byhalia, Ohio

Gene's first wife died of tuberculosis shortly after their fourth child was born. In 1930 he met Francis, who was a widow. "Gene is a real romantic," laughs Francis. "If the kids couldn't find us in the house, they knew we'd be necking out by the barn!"

※

The marriage relationship is a multifaceted, precious diamond, and among its many qualities are feelings of tender affection. If romantic passion is the sparkling brilliance of the gemstone, fondness is the fire that glows inside, the colors that shimmer deep within. And while the bright white dazzle flashes only intermittently, a close examination of the stone reveals that the colors are always there.

Find ways to show your beloved the fire that glows in your heart. Your gestures don't have to be overly creative, just simple expressions that say, "I not only love you, I really *like* you."

Sometimes it just takes a few words. Jesus communicated this sentiment to his disciples when he said, "You are my friends" (John 15:15 NLT). Sometimes all it takes is the twinkle in your eyes. Whether they are blue or green or brown, your warm look will always display the hues of your affection. And sometimes a mere touch will showcase your fondness. A squeeze of your mate's shoulder, a hand laid gently over theirs, will help show the colors in your heart.

The diamond in your spouse's wedding ring is perhaps the most visible expression of your tender feelings. Take your partner's hand, point out the fire deep in the stone, and tell them what it means.

Love one another deeply, from the heart.

1 Peter 1:22

Believe that no matter what happens, things will work out right.

Leo & Frances Jackson

Married: August 27, 1932

Gaffney, South Carolina

Leo and Frances were "married all our lives." Leo first saw Frances as she was walking down the street in front of his house. Frances says, "He grabbed his mother and pointed out the window at me and said, 'That girl's going to be my wife!'"

You and your spouse may think you have your entire life mapped out. You know where you are going, and you have figured out the way to get there. But be forewarned: You may run into delays and detours. In fact, God may ultimately have in mind for you a change in destination. Proverbs 16:9 says, "In his heart a man plans his course, but the Lord determines his steps."

It's hard to discern what is happening when things seem to go awry along our life's journey. Did we mark the map correctly? Did we make the right turn? Have we missed an important intersection? Something's wrong. Nothing looks familiar. This is not the direction we're supposed to be going. We must be lost!

When panic begins to set in, pull over for a few moments, shut off the car, and breathe a little prayer. Ask God to calm your fears and help you understand what He's doing in your life. Fold up your map, put it away, and pray for new direction, asking God to not only show you the way but ride with you and be your guide. Then turn the key, shift into gear, and head on down the highway, trusting in the Lord's goodness and in His ability to take you where He knew all along you needed to go.

"I know the plans I have for you," declares the LORD,
"plans to prosper you and not to harm you,
plans to give you hope and a future."
Jeremiah 29:11

Relax, grow old and mellow together.

Charles & Cassie Eldridge

Married: October 2, 1932

Tacoma, Maryland

Charles and Cassie met when he asked her date who she was. "He asked my boyfriend to introduce us, and that was that!" she laughs. They enjoy doing crafts together, especially making toy clowns to hand out to children.

*

The prospect of aging may seem daunting to you and your spouse. If you are prone to worry, there's plenty to be concerned about during this stage of life – as is true with every other stage. But God doesn't want you to live your life burdened with worry! He wants your minds and hearts to be at peace. So as you grow old together, relax, be lighthearted and carefree, and don't be afraid, because God has promised to look after you: "I've been carrying you on my back from the day you were born, and I'll keep on carrying you when you're old" (Isaiah 46:3-4 MSG).

Secure in this knowledge, you are free to enjoy your golden years! With age comes not only wisdom and respect but also certain privileges and opportunities, so make the most of them. Finally you have all the time you need to do the things you love to do, like gardening, woodworking, painting, sculpting, traveling, fishing, photography, writing, reading, volunteering, playing golf, making pottery – the possibilities are endless!

Just remember to take care of yourselves by eating right, getting enough sleep and exercise, and seeing the doctor regularly, so you'll both be around for a good long time and maintain a quality of life that allows you to enjoy each other – and all those grandchildren – for years to come.

Gray hair is a mark of distinction.

Proverbs 16:31 msg

A good marriage is based upon complete trust in each other.

Boyd & Carol Shafer

Married: June 6, 1932

Iowa City, Iowa

Boyd and Carol first met "in the stacks" of the university library. Boyd later became director of the American Historical Association in Washington, D.C. "We were always very close," says Carol. "I've had a very full and interesting life."

∗|∗

Children are generally trusting by nature; if they experience disappointment and hurt, however, they learn to doubt others. Likewise, young lovers often enter marriage having complete faith in one another, but a single act of disloyalty, however small, can shatter that trust, undermining and perhaps ruining the marriage relationship.

If your trust in each other remains pristine, if you feel you have no cause to doubt one another, recognize this as a true blessing! Cherish and protect that trust. It may seem rock-solid to you, but it is a fragile thing and so difficult to repair if broken.

There are many levels of unfaithfulness, ranging from the secret thoughts of the heart, to the adultery of the eyes, to the emotional infidelity of inappropriate "friendships" both in the real world and on the Internet, and all the way to physical acts of betrayal. Fight it at the heart level, and you won't have to worry about the rest. God will help you there. In fact, it's only with His help that you can win this battle.

1 Corinthians 4:2 says, "Those who have been given a trust must prove faithful." Your spouse has given you their complete trust. Don't betray it. In your actions, in your thoughts, in the depths of your heart, be completely worthy.

Let love and faithfulness never leave you; bind them around your neck, write them on the tablet of your heart.

Proverbs 3:3

Stay with it, and you can always work things out!

James "Oscar" & Beulah Scaggs

Married: September 28, 1932

Bentonville, Arkansas

Oscar and Beulah raised four children in post-Depression Arkansas. Oscar worked at the hardware store for over forty years; Beulah worked picking beans and berries and later in the cannery. "We worked different jobs," says Beulah, "but we always worked together!"

⋇

Marathon runners talk about "hitting the wall," when suddenly all energy is gone, arms and legs feel like lead, and there seems to be no way to go on. But if they press forward, forcing their bodies to perform, they eventually burst through the wall, catch their second wind, and go on to finish the race.

When you and your spouse hit a wall in your marriage, don't quit. Hebrews 12:1 says, "We must be determined to run the race that is ahead

of us" (CEV). Stay committed to the relationship and forge ahead. If it's
a brick wall and you can't break through, get creative and find a way
to go around it, climb over it, or even tunnel under it. You may have to
dismantle it brick by brick. Whatever it takes, if you work at it together,
you can move ahead.

A wise runner will take measures to ensure that when the time comes,
he will have the inner strength to conquer the wall. The day before a long
race, he will "carb out" – eat a large meal of bread, pasta, and other carbo-
hydrates that provide the body with fuel for long-term energy. You, too,
can prepare for the challenges you will face. Jesus taught His followers to
ask God for "daily bread" – physical and spiritual nourishment that would
sustain them through all adversity.

Those who hope in the LORD will renew their strength.
They will soar on wings like eagles; they will run and
not grow weary, they will walk and not be faint.

Isaiah 40:31

191

Don't disagree immediately. Discuss both sides.

Edward & Vivienne Tarr

Married: October 31, 1932

Capetown, South Africa

Edward and Vivienne met after she lost something while visiting his college. "He found my handkerchief with my name on it, and then he found me!" Vivienne says, smiling. After retiring from teaching, the couple's favorite hobby became trying out new restaurants.

In a court of law, each side has a chance to present their case. While the prosecutor is making his opening statement, questioning a witness, or giving his final argument, the defense attorney is required, for the most part, to remain silent. This way, all the known facts are brought to light and considered. Only then is a decision made.

When a dispute arises in your marriage, try a similar approach. Instead of allowing it to become a free-for-all in which you both speak at the same time, neither listening to what the other is saying, take turns presenting your viewpoints. The problem with most arguments is that nobody hears each other. Both spouses are either talking or trying to think of what to say next.

The best way to ensure that you hear and understand each other is to identify one partner as the speaker, let that person talk, then require the listener to summarize what was just said. Then it's the listener's turn to speak. If the person who has the floor is interrupted, they have the right to say politely, "Excuse me, it's my turn to talk now."

When both spouses' feelings are understood, it is much easier to reach a fair settlement. So be civil to one another when you disagree. Let's have a little order in the courtroom!

Everyone should be quick to listen, slow to speak and slow to become angry, for man's anger does not bring about the righteous life that God desires.

James 1:19-20

Work together and always help each other.

Walter & Beatrice Crandall

Married: September 15, 1932

Long Island, New York

Walter and Beatrice were editor and assistant editor of their college newspaper. "We were always together," Beatrice says. "Because we liked all the same things, marriage was a natural conclusion."

※

Are you familiar with the ropes course, the series of outdoor exercises that companies sometimes use to encourage employees to develop a sense of team spirit and camaraderie? Part of the training includes using ropes high above the ground to traverse the distance between two trees. Safety and success depends more upon teamwork and trust than on individual strength and prowess. It's a bonding experience for the participants, who learn that they can rely on their teammates to protect them, guide them, and help them prevail.

194

Perhaps every engaged couple should be required to take the ropes course as part of their premarital counseling! What a great lesson for two people to grasp as they embark on their married life together. Both would come to realize that they cannot do it on their own, they need the help of another, and their partner is on their side, standing alongside them, pulling with them to succeed.

Sometimes you have to take a risk to discover this important truth about marriage: Your partner is your *partner,* not your enemy! When you succeed, your spouse wins, and vice versa. God has put the two of you together to help one another. He's placed you on the same team, and He himself is there beside you, His hands on the ropes, ready to provide protection, guidance, and assistance.

Don't panic. I'm with you. There's no need to fear for
I'm your God. I'll give you strength. I'll help you.
I'll hold you steady, keep a firm grip on you.
Isaiah 41:10 msg

Treat each other the way you want to be treated.

Robert & Dollis Pierson

Married: September 2, 1931

Ocala, Florida

Robert and Dollis got into trouble at school a few times. "He was always moving my books over to his desk before I got to class," laughs Dollis. She adds that after they were married, he never went to sleep at night without telling her he loved her.

᠅

It's a wonder the saying, "What goes around comes around" isn't in the Bible, because God seems to have originated the concept.

Are you familiar with the story of Haman and Mordecai, found in the book of Esther? Haman was the right-hand man of the king of Persia. He hated Mordecai, a Jew who refused to honor him. So Haman plotted to kill Mordecai and all his people as well. He had a huge gallows built, planning to have Mordecai hanged on it. But through a series of amazing events, Haman was forced to honor Mordecai instead; his evil scheme was exposed; and guess who wound up on the gallows!

Haman's murderous intentions cost him his life. In a similar vein, the servant in Jesus' parable who showed no mercy found no mercy for himself. What goes around comes around. See how it works?

It's a good concept for spouses to remember. Perhaps it's the basis for the Golden Rule. Just don't devalue that precious rule, twisting it to say, "Treat others the way you've been treated." Leave the poetic justice in God's hands and focus on the positive aspects of reciprocity. Treat your spouse well, the way you want to be treated.

What goes around comes around. Hmm . . . perhaps the Bible does say that after all.

Do not judge, and you will not be judged. Do not condemn, and you will not be condemned. Forgive, and you will be forgiven. Give, and it will be given to you.

Luke 6:37-38

Life isn't always sunshine; learn to survive the storms.

Guy & Mildred Harris

Married: June 6, 1931

Nowata, Oklahoma

Guy and Mildred have lived on the same farm in northeast Oklahoma
for over half a century. Guy stays active with chores and repairs;
Mildred still cooks huge holiday meals for the family.
They're also Bill Morelan's much-loved maternal grandparents.

Jesus' disciples likely had no formal survival training. Yet when a storm threatened to overwhelm their boat and drown them all, they knew exactly what to do. They went to Jesus and asked for help. He stood up, calmed the storm, and saved them.

The apostle Paul knew whom to trust when the storm raged and shipwreck was imminent. He told the others on board, "Keep up your courage, men, for I have faith in God" (Acts 27:25). The Lord had promised him that although the ship would be lost, every person on it would survive. And so they did.

You and your spouse may have to weather real storms – hurricanes, tornadoes, powerful thunderstorms. They can be devastating and deadly. As you take proper, commonsense precautions against injury and property damage, don't forget to ask Jesus for help. Then trust God to get you through the tempest.

Figurative storms can be just as frightening and disastrous as literal ones. Sometimes an argument gets out of hand and goes unresolved for far too long. At other times you find yourselves enduring a stormy season of life, when important matters like career, family, or health get caught up in a whirlwind and the outcome seems uncertain. The means for survival are the same: go to Jesus, ask for help, and trust God.

Our God is a God who saves.

Psalm 68:20

Don't ever nag or holler at each other.

Edward & Fern Willett

Married: November 10, 1930

Washington, D.C.

Edward and Fern ran children's summer camps together for many years. "It was like a long, paid vacation every year— well, most of the time," Fern says with a grin.

※

When two people come together, it is inevitable that they will disappoint each other, for they are, after all, human. How you react to that disappointment when it comes will set the tone of your marriage. If you nag and criticize, there will be tension and hurt. If you forgive and exercise patience, the atmosphere will be a loving and peaceful one. And God has given us a good example in Jesus who forgave the world for much bigger crimes than forgetting to take out the trash or denting the car. In addition, Jesus gives us His spirit living within to help us to be just like Him in the face of disappointment.

God also holds out a wonderful promise for us. If we can learn to live together without grousing and bickering, He will make us "blameless and pure, children of God without fault," and we will "shine like stars" (Philippians 2:15) in a world that wonders what God's love really looks like.

Take advantage of what God offers. Pray for help when your spouse disappoints you. Ask for wisdom and the ability to forgive. Create a home where you love to spend time and where friends love to visit to enjoy the peace and love they feel there.

In everything you do, stay away from
complaining and arguing.
Philippians 2:14 nlt

Express your emotions and talk things out.

Frank & Alice Mosby

Married: December 7, 1929

Nashville, Tennessee

Frank and Alice were introduced by Alice's sister while Alice was visiting her in Chicago. They courted by letter and telephone for over a year. "If you don't express your emotions, you're not really being human," claims Alice.

It may be difficult for you to express your feelings at times. When you're upset, it's hard to speak what's on your mind and in your heart.

Take the time you need to gather your thoughts. And talk things over with the Lord before you try to talk them out with your spouse. God may give you insight into your own feelings and also those of your spouse. Try writing down what's going through your head, including how you feel about things. Write quickly and don't try to edit. You don't want a formal written document that you silently hand to your spouse or monotonously read to them. Just get your thoughts down; merely writing them out will help you understand what you feel. Afterward you can decide what you want to share with your partner.

However you organize your thoughts, make a decision to share what you feel and also help your spouse to feel that your marriage is a safe place to share their feelings. You both will grow closer through the experience. And even though things may be a little tense at first, working things out will create a strong peace between you and make you able to weather future difficulties.

Come now, let us reason together.

Isaiah 1:18

Stay busy – then there's no time to argue!

Carl & Oneita Johnson

Married: December 24, 1929

Siloam Springs, Arkansas

Carl and Oneita had to do their courting "by mail," since Oneita moved away after finishing school. She still has the "hope chest" she filled in the years before their marriage. "I had everything in there to start a home but the furniture!" laughs Oneita.

⋇

Puttering in the garden and tinkering in the workshop, fixing up the house and cleaning up the yard: Any useful activity is good. And when spouses stay busy, they're content – and at least they're not getting on each other's nerves. But is all this activity ultimately worthwhile?

Some of the work we do seems endlessly repetitive and meaningless at times. Making the bed, washing the dishes, mowing the grass, cleaning clothes, dusting the house – all these make our home a peaceful, orderly place. We do them all and gain a moment's satisfaction from a job well done, but in the back of our head we know we'll face these tasks again before too long. Is it all really just a waste of time?

First Corinthians 10:31 says, "Whether you eat or drink, or whatever you do, do all to the glory of God" (NKJV). Not only does useful activity keep us happy and out of trouble, it affords us the opportunity to honor the Lord. What we do has value to Him, because we have value to him. And step back and see how God uses your efforts: as the years go by, you and your spouse are maintaining a clean, safe, nurturing environment for each other and perhaps for your children. How do you calculate the value of a loving home?

Work hard and cheerfully at whatever you do,
as though you were working for the Lord.
Colossians 3:23 nlt

Settle in your heart that you're going to stick it out.

Alex & Margaret Clark

Married: November 7, 1929

Vancouver, British Columbia, Canada

Alex and Margaret spent many of their dates ice-skating.
They still have both pairs of speed skates hanging in the basement.
"Someday I'm going to have them bronzed," Alex says, grinning.

The boy stares at the mountain of debris. His parents have been
remodeling the old farmhouse, and this downstairs bedroom is a catchall,
with old building material piled nearly to the ceiling. It is time to clean,
and he gets the job. He's been working, but the mountain seems as tall
as ever. Discouraged, he calls out to his father for help. His dad answers,
"Just keep at it, Son. Remember, one piece at a time, and you'll get it
done." The boy grimaces but keeps working. A short time later his father
peeks in on him. The boy is moving slowly, but he hasn't quit. Smiling, the

man moves beside his son and without a word begins to lend him a hand. And soon the boy can see sunlight peek through the bedroom window.

Persevering in marriage requires a similar kind of decision: an act of the will to stay and get the job done. It requires determination: the resolve to keep pressing forward, one day at a time if necessary. It requires hope: the belief that endurance will reap reward. And it requires the power of a loving Father who will hear your cry, offer encouragement, and roll up his sleeves to help. So be decisive, be determined, be hopeful, and expect God's help.

I can do everything through him
who gives me strength.

Philippians 4:13

Always consider your spouse's wishes.

Frank & Rachel Spiess

Married: November 29, 1928

Washington, D.C.

Frank and Rachel met and were married while students at college. After spending over thirty years as missionaries to India, they retired to the Smoky Mountains. They deeply appreciate the beautiful scenery and country living.

"What's your desire, Queen Esther? What do you want? Ask and it's yours – even if it's half my kingdom!" (Esther 5:3 MSG).

King Xerxes may not have been the perfect role model of a husband, but he did one thing right: when his wife, Queen Esther, came to him with a special request, he listened to what she had to say. (Actually, he went a step beyond that and promised to grant his spouse's wish before he knew what it was – which may not be the wisest course of action!)

In any case, he did listen. He was pleased with his wife and valued her enough to consider her interests. He did this although he was a busy, powerful ruler, and with a wave of his hand he could have had Queen Esther swept from his presence – or much worse.

Do you heed your spouse's requests? Do you value your partner enough that you take the time to listen attentively to their desires and their wishes? Or are you only concerned about your own wants and needs, waving away your mate, dismissing their interests as unimportant and bothersome?

If you really want to feel like royalty, give your beloved the regal consideration he or she deserves, and you'll be worthy of the highest rank of nobility.

Give respect and honor to all to whom it is due.

Romans 13:7 nlt

Share common goals.

Bill & Minna Divers

Married: October 20, 1928

Cincinnati, Ohio

Bill and Minna met when they were being admitted to practice law
before the U.S. Supreme Court. "We liked the same things;
our backgrounds and educations were similar; we were very compatible."
Minna was a congressional lawyer for over thirty years; Bill's many
accomplishments are listed in the work edition of Who's Who.

One head is better than two.

That's the mystery of unity in marriage. It's not about thinking alike; it's not about putting your heads together; it's about becoming one, so you think as one. That is, as you set important goals for your marriage – as you make weighty choices about your career, your home, your family, and other matters – you begin with the same core values, principles, and beliefs. You are both involved in the deliberation process, and when you reach a unified decision, you are both at peace with it, and you both own it completely. There will be no selfish pride or finger pointing later as the consequences of your decision unfold, both good and bad.

Unity is vital to a marriage. As a married couple, the last thing you want is to be pulling in opposite directions! But unity isn't handed to a man and woman when they are presented to the community as man and wife; it is a growing together that happens over time. Yes, God made you one when you took your vows, but still you must strive together for oneness. That's part of the mystery.

So work toward unity in your relationship. Wait for it, especially when making important decisions and setting goals. Ask God to guide your thinking. He made you one; He can create unity between you as well.

Be united in what you think,
as if you were only one person.
Philippians 2:2 cev

Make love and trust the cornerstones of your marriage.

Henry & Mary Lankford

Married: August 21, 1928

Gentry, Arkansas

Henry first saw Mary on a farm where he was spraying the orchard. A few weeks later he asked if he could walk her home from a church meeting. "A marriage isn't much," says Mary, "unless it's based on true love and trust."

⁂

The little girl was growing frustrated. She was trying to stack her wooden alphabet blocks atop one another on the carpet, but every time her tower began to rise, it would wobble and fall over. Finally her mother knelt beside her, saying, "Let me show you a little trick." She put four of the blocks together to make a foundation and said, "Now, build your tower on this." The little girl began to stack her blocks on top of it, and she squealed with delight as the tower rose higher and higher – until her mother had to pick her up to place the last one.

212

As you envision that little girl's engineering feat and consider it in relation to your marriage, notice the letters on the four cornerstones: L, T, C, and F. The first two represent *love* – selfless, patient, humble, forgiving, hopeful, kind, unfailing – and *trust,* which is rock-solid as long as it is cherished and protected. Both are essential to your relationship.

The third block, C, stands for *commitment,* the resolution to keep your wedding vows at all costs. It's the cornerstone that supports security – and, ironically, freedom – and it stands side by side with *trust.* Finally, the fourth block, F, represents *faith.* It is the chief cornerstone, the one that unites the entire structure so that it stands straight and tall.

Take some time to think about how you can use these cornerstones in your marriage.

God is building a home . . . He's using you, fitting you
in brick by brick, stone by stone, with Christ Jesus
as the cornerstone that holds all the parts together.
Ephesians 2:19-21 msg

Spend time looking for ways to help each other.

Paul & Phyllis Current

Married: June 15, 1927

Sand Point, Idaho

Paul and Phyllis always tried to put God first in their lives. "We once bought an abandoned schoolhouse," says Phyllis, "and remodeled it into a church." Paul ran a small sawmill operation; Phyllis worked as an art teacher and landscape artist.

※

Spouses have a tremendous potential and opportunity to help one another, from simple acts of service, like preparing lunch, to great deeds of encouragement and support, such as helping a mate find the fortitude to leave a secure but unfulfilling job and start a new career.

God gives people various talents, skills, and abilities, which He wants us to use in service to others. Some of these are listed in the Bible as "spiritual gifts." They include serving, teaching, encouraging, giving, leading, showing mercy, having wisdom and possessing faith. These are powerful tools, which the Lord has placed in our hands to help others – and that certainly includes our spouse.

Think of the many other proficiencies people exercise – each of which could be used to assist a spouse. Some organize well; others have a good head for business; some are artistic and creative; others communicate well; some have wonderful social skills; others are gifted mechanics; some are fantastic homcmakers; others have great physical strength, computer skills, financial aptitudes, mathematical talents, scientific acumen – the list goes on.

Take the time to get to know yourself and what you have to offer, and consider ways in which you could use your gifts to help the one you love.

Carry each other's burdens, and in this
way you will fulfill the law of Christ.

Galatians 6:2

You've got to have love, and you've got to know God.

Floyd & Mary Dixon

Married: April 1, 1923

Fallsville, Arkansas

Floyd and Mary met while riding horses along the Buffalo River
in Arkansas. Floyd ran a sawmill; the nearest town had less than
a dozen homes. "I only worked for money once," Mary says, smiling.
"That was so I could buy a new cookstove. After I bought it,
Floyd said, 'Now you don't need to work anymore.'"

※

David Livingstone spent years traveling through Africa, trying to discover the source of the mighty Nile River, and died without ever finding it. However, with the Bible's help, in two steps we can locate not only the source but also the essence of a much greater river, Love.

Ready for our expedition? Here we go: 1 John 4:7 states, "Love comes from God," and 1 John 4:16 says, "God is love." So there you have it. We've traced love to its source, and it's no great mystery. Love originates with God, and the essence of love is God's very nature.

It almost goes without saying that to have a good marriage, you've got to have love. But how many people understand that to have love, you've got to go to the Source?

There's a great danger in our society today, because people have made love their destination, as if it were the wellspring of everything they needed. But that's akin to walking along the ocean shore, reaching the mouth of a grand river, and announcing, "Eureka! I've found the source of all this water!" For Dr. Livingstone, the river was just the starting point.

The River Love is majestic, its waters intoxicating, its fountain divine. But go further. Look for the Source; you won't have to search for long.

Let us love one another, for love comes from God.
Everyone who loves has been born of God and knows God.

1 John 4:7

Develop similar interests.

Charles & Mary Dresbach

Married: November 8, 1926

Amarillo, Texas

Charles and Mary traveled the globe together in his work as a geologist. "Charles was so patient," Mary says. "At first we had lots of disagreements, but he would always overlook them." Mary eventually fell in love with travel and even learned to like geology. "And then we had a lot more to talk about!" she says.

As you foster similar interests as a couple, be sure to engage in the most important pursuit of all: getting to know God. He is infinite – and there are endless rewards in pursuing Him. This is one activity every couple should be involved in together! Two good places to start are God's Word, which is the Bible, and God's people, which is the Church.

There are guides available to help you study the Bible together at home. Or you could join a couples Bible study group, which provides social interaction and lets you learn from other people about the scriptures. The Bible is a rich book, full of life-changing truths, and probing its depths takes a lifetime. You and your spouse will be rewarded with many meaningful conversations and experiences as you share the insights and discoveries you glean from its pages.

Attending church together weekly is one of the best steps you can take in your quest to know God. It allows you to worship together and build relationships with God's people. Get involved somehow, perhaps by joining a small group that interests you or by volunteering to serve in some capacity.

God reveals Himself through His Word and His people, providing you both with knowledge and real-life experience. Seek Him together!

Let us go to the house of the LORD.

Psalm 122:1 nlt

Choose a neat and tidy partner – it certainly makes life easier!

Ray & Vernal Augenstein

Married: October 14, 1926

Waldo, Ohio

Vernal kept the house spotless, while Ray maintained an immaculate yard. When Ray passed away, Vernal never remarried, because "I could never find a man as neat as him."

⚜

Is cleanliness really next to godliness? It depends on how you define the word *clean*.

The outside of a home may look fantastic, but what if the inside is a mess? You can power-wash the exterior of a house and make it look great, but at day's end you'll pack up your equipment and head indoors. The condition of the interior is more important, because that's where you really live.

220

The Bible makes it clear that God is more concerned with what's inside us than with what shows on the outside. 1 Samuel 16:7 says, "Men and women look at the face; God looks into the heart" (MSG). To God, character is more important than outward appearance.

When considering someone for marriage, you'd be wise to adopt God's priorities. It's wonderful if the person you're interested in drives a clean car and keeps their place nice and tidy. It's great if this person keeps in shape, dresses well, and is always nicely groomed. Neat habits are a good sign that people care about themselves enough to take care of themselves. But a good-hearted person will care about you as well.

Perform a white-glove inspection on *all* the qualities of the one you're thinking of marrying. Closely examine the person's character. And when you do, look deeply into their heart – that's where you'll really live.

Who may ascend the hill of the Lord?
Who may stand in his holy place?
He who has clean hands and a pure heart.
Psalm 24:3-4

Don't fuss about every little thing. Work on being agreeable.

Cecil & Nola Critchfield

Married: May 12, 1926

Chandler, Oklahoma

Cecil and Nola first met as children but weren't married until they were in their twenties. Cecil spent most of his life working for telephone and electric companies. "We never had much," says Nola, "but we always had each other!"

※

Jesus had a humorous way of telling people to focus on self-improvement rather than on fixing others' imperfections. He said, "Why worry about a speck in your friend's eye when you have a log in your own?" (Matthew 7:3 NLT). He didn't mean it literally, of course; He meant we should do our best to correct the wrongs we do, and not be so concerned about changing others' bad behavior.

This is good advice for married couples, first of all because it works! The only person who can change you is you, and the only one who can change your spouse is your spouse. If both of you focus on changing each other, you'll get nowhere. But if each of you focuses on altering your own behavior – voilà! Presto chango!

Think of it this way: If your partner really did have a speck of sawdust in his or her eye, it would be unwise for you to reach in and try to extract it. The best way to get it out would be for your mate to bend over, look down, and blink several times, allowing the tears to flush it out.

So ask God to help you to courageously face your own weaknesses as He shows them to you. And let God deal with your partner – He will! Then you will both see eye to eye.

Do your part to live in peace with everyone,
as much as possible.
Romans 12:18 nlt

A good marriage is give and take – but mostly give.

Merywn & Freda Bridenstine

Married: June 25, 1925

Iowa City, Iowa

Merywn and Freda met in college and later developed teaching careers. "We never had a serious fight," says Merywn. "In almost every situation, we both gave instead of insisting on our own way."

⁂

You possess an incredible gift that you can give your spouse. In fact, you own a vast array of gifts that you can bestow on your partner. The choice is yours. Will you keep the gifts locked up and hidden away, or will you joyfully and willingly present them to your mate as an expression of your love?

The asset to which you hold the title, the gift that only you can give, is yourself. Examine the contents of the box before you wrap it, and you'll discover that there are many little gifts, individually wrapped, waiting to be shared. These are the gifts of time, effort, attention, openness, respect, patience, humility, kindness, touch, laughter, thoughtfulness, romance, acceptance, sacrifice, and compromise.

The gift of yourself truly is one that keeps on giving. If you are willing to give yourself fully and completely to your spouse, then each day, year after year, your mate will be thrilled to have packages to open, providing them with a lifetime of joy and contentment. Your spouse's gratitude and appreciation for your gift will last just as long, and will manifest itself in the quality of your relationship.

Your spouse will have packages for you to open as well, to be sure; but for now simply enjoy the sparkle of happiness in your beloved's eyes, and bask in the pure joy of giving.

My own vineyard is mine to give.

Song of Songs 8:12

Don't expect everything in your marriage to be perfect.

Russell & Virginia Potter Sr.

Married: May 27, 1924

Elkhart, Indiana

*Russell and Virginia owned and operated hardware stores
for over half a century. Even though Russell Sr. is now in
his nineties, they still drive to church together every week!*

❋

"Once upon a time, they lived happily ever after."

There it is – the world's shortest fairy tale. A bit lacking in detail, but it kind of captures the essence of all fairy tales, doesn't it? The dreamy, romantic quality, the perfect, blissful ending – just right for bedtime story-books, but as it turns out, not such a good model for marriages!

You and your spouse have to live out your "ever after" in the real world, where things don't always go so smoothly. That's okay, as long as your expectations are in line with reality. The problem is, many of us cling to fairy-tale notions about married life, expect our partners to live up to them, and experience bitter disappointment and resentment when, despite all our wishing on stars, our dreams don't exactly come true.

So for the sake of our marriages, it's time to say goodbye to Never-Never Land. It's time to embrace life as it really is and grapple with its challenges. It's time to see our spouses as they really are, and not complain when the glass slipper falls off.

But must we give up all our dreams? For believers, the answer is no. We simply look toward heaven and place our faith, our hope for eternal joy, in something more powerful than a wish.

I, Jesus, . . . [am] the Bright Morning Star.

Revelation 22:16 msg

Heartwarmers

Lie on a blanket in the sun
and just melt together.

Walk along the shore
in the moonlight.

Light candles and listen
to romantic music.

When faced with a mistake, forgive and go on.

Ollie & Hattie Sisk

Married: December 1, 1924

Westville, Oklahoma

Ollie and Hattie went to school together in a one-room country schoolhouse.
"We used to make music together," says Hattie.
"Ollie had a guitar, and I played an old pump-organ." Hattie still remembers
the moment Ollie sat her under a tree and said,
"I want you to be my wife someday." She was thirteen at the time.

※

Does your spouse have a criminal record? Do the local authorities or the FBI have a file with your partner's name on it? It may be that your answer to these questions is yes. Perhaps your spouse made a mistake, served time in prison, and now is a free citizen, their crime paid for. They have been given another chance and been reintegrated into society. This is how our justice system handles wrong behavior.

How do you deal with your spouse's mistakes? Do you forgive and forget? Do you resist keeping a detailed file of your partner's wrongs, pulling out papers and waving them accusingly every time a new argument arises? It is tempting to keep adding to that record until your file cabinet begins to bulge, isn't it? We all struggle with letting go of past hurts.

We know that love doesn't keep accounts of past hurts. It's a little like the justice system, which provides a second chance to the offender and restores them. But it's even *more* like God's system, which is characterized by grace. There is no debt to be paid, because the one who loves is willing to "take the hit" for the offense, forgive, and burn the record.

Take a look at your heart and be willing to burn past records and forgive. After the smoke clears, the air of your marriage will be clear.

Love is not irritable, and it keeps no record
of when it has been wronged.

1 Corinthians 13:5 nlt

Your roles must be clearly defined.

Roy & Cody Derry
Married: November 26, 1924
First View, Colorado

Cody believes the ideal marriage is one in which "the husband is a loving boss and the wife his willing partner." She says her husband Roy fit that ideal perfectly. "He was so handsome, so smart, and so nice to me that I never even thought of leaving!"

✢

Dance lessons ought to be a requirement for premarital counseling. Any couple who can survive the lessons is ready for marriage!

In ballroom dancing, the man is the designated leader. It is his job to guide his partner around the floor, indicating which way she is to go and when she is to turn. The woman's assignment is to follow her partner's lead, complementing his moves, her weight counterbalancing his as they glide through a series of twirls.

Without this clear delineation of roles, without leadership and submission, cooperation and communication, the couple would not float "effortlessly" about; they would trip over each other and fall unceremoniously to the dance floor!

Dancing is not some kind of competition between the partners. Rather, it is an art form in which two people unite and strive together to achieve a height of artistic, emotional, and spiritual expression they could never reach alone. It is the perfect picture of a marriage.

A good leader does not bully his partner, pushing and pulling her across the floor. He guides her gently and considerately, watching over her shoulder to protect her. His strength supports her beauty and grace; she trusts him and willingly follows his lead because she can depend on his love. Make your marriage a dance of love.

The husband provides leadership to his wife the way Christ does to his church, not by domineering but by cherishing.

Ephesians 5:23 msg

Take time to work through your problems.

Kimball & Genevieve Slaugh

Married: January 3, 1924

Logan, Utah

Because of his work with the federal government, Kimball and Genevieve faced the stress of moving often. "We've lived in such diverse places as Iran and Vietnam," says Genevieve. "It's been an interesting, and at times challenging, way of life."

☙

Marital difficulties may seem like raging floodwaters when you and your spouse are struggling in the midst of them. You may begin to panic, fearing that you will be overwhelmed. But remember that you are not fighting the deluge alone. God has promised, "When you pass through the waters, I will be with you; and when you pass through the rivers, they will not sweep over you" (Isaiah 43:2). Trust the Lord's promise, call out to Him, and cling to Him. He'll take you safely to high ground.

As He carries you both along through the swift current, you can rest in His arms, secure in His protection and in the commitment you share with your spouse. Now you can discuss with your partner how you came to be in such dire circumstances and begin to work out a solution to the problem, looking for changes each of you can make so you'll never wander into this type of danger again.

Invite God into the dialogue. You can't see Him, but He's there; you feel His strong arms supporting you through the crisis, even now rescuing you. As He conveys you to shelter, He will whisper words of wisdom if you seek His input and listen. And when at last He sets you down, alive and well, thank Him and ask Him to stay.

Many waters cannot quench love;
rivers cannot wash it away.

Song of Songs 8:7

You can always work things out if you really want to.

Earl & Ila McNair

Married: October 16, 1921

Siloam Springs, Arkansas

Earl and Ila met at a food booth during the city picnic.
After they were married, Earl opened a plumbing business
while Ila raised their two children and helped out in the shop.
"If you can't get along before *you're married," Ila advises,*
"you sure won't manage with the added pressures of a job and children!"

⁜

If your marriage seems hopeless, remember that "no one whose hope is in [the LORD] will ever be put to shame" (Psalm 25:3). Hope truly does spring eternal, if it wells up from the Source of all real hope. Never give in. Renew your commitment to your spouse, hold your ground, and keep trusting in God.

When things are at their worst, you may be tempted not only to give up hope but also to question your very faith. You might wonder why a good God would allow you to suffer such awful circumstances, when you've done your best to obey Him. But the Bible says that once we are in God's hands, He will never let us go. Our faith may be tested, but He won't allow it to die.

In bad times, you may start to fear that your love for your spouse, or their love for you, has grown cold. There seems to be nothing left between you except emptiness. But like hope and faith, love never dies completely. If you and your spouse keep trusting in God despite every reason to quit, He will prove himself trustworthy. He will rekindle the embers in your hearts and fan the flames until they once again burn steady and strong. So trust God, even when you don't understand His ways.

There are three things that will endure—faith, hope, and love—and the greatest of these is love.
1 Corinthians 13:13 nlt

Work at becoming closer and closer.

Elmer & Emma Porter

Married: June 21, 1921

Oklahoma City, Oklahoma

Emma first met Elmer while he was working in a friend's barbershop. "He seemed so nice and was nice-looking, too!" she recalls. Elmer eventually owned his own barbershop, while Emma worked in a nearby grocery store. "We enjoyed just being together," says Emma.

⋇

Dressing to the nines, renting a limousine, buying your spouse roses and champagne, and treating your beloved to a wonderful night on the town may foster feelings of romance, but if you want to experience true intimacy, you must first plumb the depths of Christ's love, then give your spouse a love that runs as close to those depths as possible.

In addition, the journey toward intimacy with your spouse lies along the pathway of obedience to God. We are commanded to love each other as Jesus loves us. That's a tall order, because Christ not only loves us with a pure, selfless love; He also sacrificed Himself willingly on our behalf. The Bible says that no one has greater love than he who gives his life for another. We can never love each other as much as Jesus loves us, but we are called to spend our lives emulating that love.

Think about it. What would loving your spouse like Jesus loves them look like? What would you do to reach that kind of love? If it means flowers, do it. If it means picking up dirty laundry, encouraging them, or giving them a quiet moment at the end of the day, do it.

My command is this: love each other
as I have loved you.

John 15:12

Always treat each other well.

Theopolis & Martha Johnson

Married: December 24, 1915

Gravette, Arkansas

On their wedding day, Theopolis and Martha (Thee and Mattie)
were accompanied by her sister. Not knowing the family, the pastor
asked which girl was the bride. "Oh, it don't make no difference,"
joked Thee. "They're both kinda pretty, don't you think?"
"I hit him," laughs Mattie, "and then we were married."

⁂

What first attracted you to your spouse? What do you find compelling about your partner today? Physical attraction often plays a significant role in drawing a couple together early in their relationship. Over time, however, the importance of eye appeal declines; rising in prominence to take its place is another type of allure: inner beauty.

But how is the loveliness of one's character exhibited? The answer is, it's displayed through a person's behavior. Our words and actions flow from our hearts.

In discussing how spouses ought to behave, the apostle Peter looked beyond how they should present themselves, even looked past what they should do and say. He addressed the core of the issue: "What matters is not your outer appearance – the styling of your hair, the jewelry you wear, the cut of your clothes – but your inner disposition. Cultivate inner beauty, the gentle, gracious kind that God delights in" (1 Peter 3:3-4 MSG). In other words, don't focus on how you look or act; focus on who you are. That's where beauty and behavior begin.

God can help you cultivate inner beauty, molding your character and making you more like Jesus – the most beautiful one of all. As He does, you'll treat your spouse better. And you'll develop an attractiveness that will never fade.

When you look in the mirror, be sure to check for inner beauty too.

You wives: Be good wives to your husbands, responsive to their needs. . . . You husbands: Be good husbands to your wives. Honor them, delight in them.

1 Peter 3:1, 7 msg

241

Ask yourself what God would have you do.

Art& Angie Grumbine

Married: February 5, 1944

Tujunga, California

Art and Angie say the secret for a long marriage is the same as for
any other decision: "Ask yourself what God would have you do."

※

Many divorces occur because people suddenly feel a need to run off
and find themselves. But that's not the way God wants us to discover who
we are and what His intention for us is. The Lord controls every situation,
and if we are serious about learning our purpose and identity, we must
consider our circumstances.

If you are a married man, the Bible clearly says that God wants you
to be a husband. If you have children, He wants you to be a parent. If
you are a married woman, God wants you to be a wife. Our identity and

purpose do not end with these roles, but they are a core component of God's will.

The Bible must be the place we run to find ourselves. It's where God has expressly stated His will. We cannot bend His laws to conform to our needs and desires; we must conform ourselves to His will and rely on Him to meet our needs. When we do, we'll be amazed to discover the incredible value of our true identity, and what amazing, eternally significant purposes God has in mind for us.

So when trouble makes you wonder what you should do, look to God for instructions.

Don't copy the behavior and customs of this world,
but let God transform you into a new person
by changing the way you think. Then you will know
what God wants you to do, and you will know
how good and pleasing and perfect his will really is.

Romans 12:2 nlt

Talk and pray your way through problems.

Delbert & Wanda Wilkins

Married: January 9, 1943

Lawton, Oklahoma

"You can talk and pray your way through most problems,"
says Wanda. "And you don't have to say everything
that you're thinking," Delbert adds with a laugh.

※

When you were a child, there was nothing your dad couldn't do. There was no problem he couldn't handle, no plaything he couldn't fix. Circumstances never got so bad that he couldn't take care of things. You simply went to him and asked for help, and he got up from his chair, analyzed the situation, and went to work. Dad could do anything!

As you grew older, you began to realize there were limitations to your father's prowess. But hopefully he or someone else taught you that when things get to be too much for even dear old Dad, there is someone else you can turn to: your Father in heaven. He loves you dearly, has unlimited ability, wants to help, and is simply waiting for you to ask.

You and your spouse are sure to encounter many problems in your marriage, both small and big. Communication is a powerful tool to help you fix them, but don't rely on your own proficiency as you try to make repairs. Get some help. Your heavenly Father says, "I am the LORD, the God of all mankind. Is anything too hard for me?" (Jeremiah 32:27). He can take your hand as you struggle to use the tool of communication. Lending His wisdom and strength, He will enable you to achieve amazing results.

If you are having trouble, you should pray.

James 5:13 cev

Work together toward common goals.

Joseph & Lenora Holland

Married: November 2, 1939

Watts, Oklahoma

Joseph and Lenora are "complete opposites in disposition"
yet have learned to work together toward common goals.
"You must always love and appreciate each other," says Lenora.

※

World-class athletes know that it takes focus, effort, and sacrifice to achieve any goal that is truly worthwhile. This is true for solo competition as well as team sports. The latter, however, also requires cooperation and communication. Team members not only work hard together but also communicate with one another to provide information, feedback, and especially encouragement.

You and your spouse are a team, and you will have to cooperate and communicate with each other as you strive for victory. You'll need to talk things over as you choose which goals to pursue and decide how you will achieve them. You'll need to keep each other informed as you assume your individual roles and execute your unique assignments. You'll need to compare notes as you evaluate your progress. And you'll need to encourage one another as you work hard, reminding each other to keep your eyes on the prize and never give up.

Encouragement is such an important component of the communication between teammates because it delivers hope and renews energy, inspiring fresh enthusiasm, dedication, and commitment. Words of encouragement can literally make the difference between failure and success.

With a little encouragement from each other – and a little help from the Lord – you'll soon be rejoicing together that you've accomplished your goals, and your communication will take the tone of celebration.

Encourage one another daily, as long as it is called Today.

Hebrews 3:13

Make it right, even if you weren't at fault.

Ralph & Dorothy Gustin

Married: November 6, 1937

Spokane, Washington

Today Ralph and Dorothy's favorite pastime is working needlepoint. "Just give us some yarn, and we're happy," Dorothy says, laughing.

>\|<

If you grew up with siblings, you know how contentious family life can be. At times there is such animosity among brothers and sisters. Yet at other times they coexist peacefully, enjoying each other, doing things together happily. At such times it's a joy to be part of the family, and the home is a pleasant place.

When God looks down on a husband and wife, He sees two of his children living together. If they fight, He is not so much concerned with pointing out who is to blame as He is with healing the relationship and restoring peace to the home. Revealing who is at fault is not the first thing on God's agenda. He knows who did wrong – in most cases, it's both partners – and He's willing to take the blame Himself if allowed. Because of Jesus' sacrifice for our sins, God can render the issue of which spouse bears the guilt null and void, from His perspective. And since His perspective is the only one that really matters, all that remains is for the couple to forgive one another and reconcile.

When you and your spouse argue, don't get hung up on determining who's at fault. Even if you know in your heart you were not to blame, don't focus on what went wrong; do whatever you can to make things right.

How wonderful, how beautiful,
when brothers and sisters get along!
Psalm 133:1 msg

Do not hesitate to express to each other your feelings and your love.

William Harold & Bessie Lee Jackson

Married: March 28, 1937

Plano, Texas

Bessie Lee and William had known each other two and a half years before they married. "From the evening we met we had a very devoted, romantic, loving, platonic courtship. There was never much doubt as to where our love would lead," William says. "Our pledges to each other have been kept. Our loving, romantic courtship is still alive."

⚘

John 3:16 says, "God so loved the world that he gave his one and only Son, that whoever believes in him shall not perish but have eternal life." When our heavenly Father wanted to express His love, He gave up what was most precious to Him: His Son, Jesus. Christ in turn gave up His life to reveal His love.

250

Are you willing to give up everything for your spouse? If the need arose, would you be willing to die for them? Perhaps you would. For most of us, though, there is a more pressing question, and we are called to give up our life in a different way, one that may be even harder. The question is, Are you willing to live for your spouse? Are you willing to pour out your life each day for the sake of your beloved?

If the greatest expression of love is self-sacrifice, then God and Jesus have set the standard. They have raised the bar to the highest level. Our greatest response to Their sacrificial love for us is to reciprocate, loving Them both with all our being and giving of ourselves for Their sake. Love is also to sacrifice for the one whom They cherish beyond measure – your spouse.

So, are you willing to give your life for your spouse? Start now.

This is how God showed his love among us: He sent his one and only Son into the world that we might live through him.

1 John 4:9

If you have enjoyed this book,

Hallmark would love

to hear from you.

Please send comments to:

Hallmark Book Feedback

P.O. Box 419034

Mail Drop 215

Kansas City, MO 64141

Or e-mail us at:

booknotes@hallmark.com